His Everlasting Love

Stories of the Father's Help to His Children

Norma Clark Larsen

INTERNATIONAL STANDARD BOOK NUMBER
0-88290-083-8

LIBRARY OF CONGRESS CATALOG CARD NUMBER
77-79752

Second Printing July 1979

Printed in the
United States of America
by
**Horizon Publishers
& Distributors
P.O. Box 490
50 South 500 West
Bountiful, Utah 84010**

To my beloved parents

Jonah and Estella Frisbey Clark

and

my "Second Parents," my brother and sister:

L. Eldon Clark and LaRee Arend Doxey

with sincere gratitude and love.

ACKNOWLEDGEMENTS

I wish to express my appreciation to those who have contributed to the formation of this book by giving me help and assistance, encouragement, stories, and permission to use their own or a relative's experiences.

My "thank you" goes to the following who encouraged me to try, and gave suggestions on how to approach this task: President Milton W. Russon, Bishop William Pace, Helen and Monte Larsen, June and Steve Call and many others.

A special thanks to Donna Harston who obtained permission to use many stories other than her own, who encouraged and supported me in numerous ways, and who also closely followed the progress of the book. To Winnifred Harris of St. George, Utah, the daughter of Maggie Tolman Porter whose many stories are included in this book, I wish to express gratitude to her for permission to use "Maggie's" stories which are all filled with inspiration.

To Duane S. Crowther of Horizon Publishers, who has contributed so much to the arranging, finishing, and polishing of this book, I wish to express my sincere appreciation and thanks. I know that without his exceptional help, patience and kindness it would not have been possible to bring this work to a conclusion.

To my family: Justine (Julia), Clark, Emory, Bruce, Douglas, Paula, Joyce and Ross, who patiently listened to stories and revisions and offered suggestions and encouragement, I want to express love and appreciation.

With the greatest joy and with a heart full of love and appreciation, I wish to thank my Father in Heaven who contributed inspiration, encouragement and at times direct suggestions and revisions on the material of this book. Without His promise of help and His statement, "Writing this book is a good thing," I probably would never have started this book at all. May this book be a means of encouraging others to come closer to our Father that they might receive His help in all things!

Norma Clark Larsen

TABLE OF CONTENTS

Chapter One

GOD ANSWERS PRAYERS THROUGH REVEALED WORDS

Our Heavenly Father shows His love in all that He does for us. He has provided all things needful for us—our earthly home, our parents, food, clothing, work, the beauties of nature, and guidance in all things through the gospel and through His servants. He provided a Savior for us, His beloved Son, Jesus Christ. The apostle John wrote that "He that loveth not, knoweth not God, for God is love. In this was manifested the love of God toward us, because that God sent His only begotten Son into the world, that we might live through Him. Herein is love, not that we loved God, but that He loved us, and sent His Son to be the propitiation for our sins." (Jn. 4:8-10.)

Each day God is giving gifts of love to us; answers to prayers, guidance, protection, spiritual joy, healing when ill, protection from evil influences, and help with all of life's problems. President Marion G. Romney has observed that:

In these uneasy days of fearful suspense and tragedy, there is comfort and strength in the knowledge that God is our Heavenly Father, that He is not a distant, indefinable abstraction, but a loving and understanding parent, so near that we can have daily communication with Him. He can reach each of us with His strengthening and protecting power.

That we may have the desire and the courage and the humility to gain that knowledge and enjoy the fruits thereof, is my humble prayer. ("God Is Not Far From Us," *Ensign*, August, 1976, p. 4)

In the January 1976 issue of the *Ensign* there were many beautiful and thought provoking articles on prayer which impressed me deeply and touched my heart. When President Romney wrote that "I know what Enos meant when he said, 'the voice of the Lord came into my mind again.' (Enos 10). By this means I have received in sentences answers to my prayers." (p 5). I was moved once more to tears of gratitude to the Father. In his article, "Prayer and The Prophet Joseph," Truman Madsen observed that "Half at least of the prayer process is bringing our souls into receptivity so that we may be powerful listeners and learn the how and when and what of prayer." (p 20) Francine Bennion's article, "Stone or Bread" mentions people who "bear moving testimony of direct daily help in problem solving," which includes help in choosing a mate, occupation, or even in finding lost articles.

God's help and concern for His children is an on-going activity while He is offering guidance to every person on the earth. He literally holds our lives in His hand. Nevertheless, He gives us the option of accepting or rejecting His help. We can obey His commandments and reap the benefits, or disobey them and lose the blessings. Our free agency is involved and our freedom to choose is necessary to our growth and progress.

The Lord has said that He will open the windows of heaven and pour out blessings upon us, until we cannot contain them, *if* we will keep the commandments and *if* we will ask. The Lord was referring specifically to tithes when He made this promise in Malachi 3:10, but it is also applicable to keeping all of His commandments, because we indeed gain great blessings when we obey Him; never have we obeyed the Lord without reaping blessings. This principle is explained in the Doctrine and Covenants, Section 82:10, where the Master pledges "I the Lord am bound when ye do what I say; when ye do not what I say, ye have no promise."

The Father wants us to pray to him always and to keep *all* the commandments and in turn He will give us *all* the help that we need to return to His presence.

Prayer is the key to the receiving of God's guidance. His answers come in many ways, as will be shown in this and the following chapters. Often, the answer to prayer comes through actual words spoken to the recipient aloud or within the confines of his mind. This chapter shares a number of incidents in which specific words were revealed in answer to prayerful requests.

How Prayer Has Guided My Life

From as far back as I can remember I have known that my Father in Heaven was close to me and would help me in the many situations where His guidance and protection was needed.

My father died when I was three years of age. When I was six years old, I went to live with a brother, then with a sister. During the years which followed they tried to make the Lord and the gospel a great part of my life, for which I am eternally grateful. They were choice people, these two, and their example of righteous living set my feet on the right path while I was young enough to heed their advice. I seemed to know that the Lord's designs for me were to help me seek the goal of eternal life if I would but keep the commandments and ask for guidance each day. Time and again He aided me, and with childish faith I called on Him often and felt secure.

My patriarchal blessing, which was full of beautiful promises, increased my reliance on the Lord for guidance during my teen years. Maybe I was foolish at times, but my desire to keep the Lord's commandments grew with the years, and I knew that He wanted that which was best for me and I would repent my childish follies and try again. I think it was at this time that I could see the security that comes with holding fast to the Lord's hand and I could not envision a life without Him beside me.

The Lord guided me into a temple marriage with the "right" man. During the following years that we raised our nine children, He helped us often with our problems as we attempted to teach our family the way of life that we knew would bring salvation and happiness to them. Secure is the word—we were secure in the knowledge that no matter what problems might arise, the Lord was beside us and would help us through our trials and tribulations. I am grateful to Him— grateful that I knew He was there, helping us and showing us the right answer to the difficulties of daily living. No, He did not remove all our problems, He just helped us to solve them. I began to say, "Problems exist to be solved," and added,... "with the Lord's help."

Many an answer came with an assurance that a certain course was the right one to take. However, many difficulties were no doubt averted by pre-problem prayers which asked for direction to do the right thing in the first place. Fear and doubts about decisions came at times, but with further prayer, solutions came, too, which we thankfully received and tried to implement.

My husband passed away in 1964 after a brief illness which became apparent when he fainted from loss of blood and was hospitalized with a bleeding ulcer. This was to be complicated by blood clots which claimed his life less than a month later. The Lord was beside me to comfort and support me in days that followed as I learned to accept my husband's death and the loss of his companionship. Certainly the Father helped me to raise our children who at this time ranged in age from six to twenty-four. It wasn't difficult to adjust to the new situation because a wise husband had tried to keep us as debt free as possible, so we managed fine.

The most important blessing of all came into my life at this time, for the Lord began to compensate for the loss of my priesthood leadership by increasing His help to us. Surprisingly, I began to get much more explicit instructions from the Lord in the form of words and sentences which came as answers to my questions, or sometimes came as verification or rejection of my own decisions. I was amazed, but had very little trouble accepting these answers. I became aware that increased guidance was coming because I needed more help at this time and that this was the Lord's special way of helping me.

Now I see that all of us need more help from the Lord. Sometimes we are unsure if these answers are from the Lord or from our own minds, but if we will stay close to the Lord and keep His commandments, along with revealed answers will come feelings of assurance which cannot be duplicated in any other way. With experience, I was able to stop my mind from running around in circles and giving to me my own answers. I held it tightly in rein while I listened intently, sometimes almost holding my breath, so I would not begin thinking my own answers. When I was sure of the answer, I learned never to doubt it at a later time. The Lord helped me with that principle, because at one time I went back and asked Him if the answer was from Him or perhaps I had made it up and

He said, "You believed Me when I told you." This second verification has served as a constant reminder to me: never doubt, once you know the answer is from the Lord. Also strengthening me was a scriptural sentence I found one day in Enos, verse ten: "The voice of the Lord came into my mind saying...." and I shouted with joy, "Yes, yes, yes, that is the way the Lord answers, isn't it?" And I blessed Enos.

One day in a Sunday School class we were discussing prayer and the Lord's way of answering us. I was delighted when Ronald Prows told of a suggestion put to him by his friend, Brother Truman Madsen: "Ron, when you pray, do you listen? Afterwards, get up and write down what you hear." Following class, I stopped him and asked, "Do you do this?" "Yes," he shyly admitted, "but I seem to get more answers when I ask about my students than when I ask about my own children." I thought, that is because he needs more help with the students, whereas with his own children he feels more adequate to find solutions and does not need as much help. Another brother, mindful that the Lord requires work and perserverance on our part in order that we may accomplish life's goals, said, "I do all I can first, then I call on the Lord for help." I later asked him, "Do you say your prayers in the morning each day?" to which he answered, "Yes, of course." "Well then, don't you think that you are not giving the Lord enough credit for His help? While you are working and persevering, He is already helping you and when you run into serious problems you can ask for 'extra' help." He agreed with me. This exchange caused me to realize that the Lord is giving us much help of which we are not fully aware. It also helped me to be more appreciative of His protective care.

If we sincerely want to live for His blessings, and if we want to get closer to our Father in Heaven and be more certain of His answers, I have found the following attitudes may be helpful in receiving answers to our prayers:

1. Have faith,
2. Know that those things the Lord wants for us are best for us,
3. Believe the Lord's decisions are superior to our own,
4. Be willing to accept problems for growth,
5. Know that the Lord wants us to learn unselfishness, grow spiritually, gain maturity, and serve our fellow man,

6. Tell the Lord that you truly need and want help,
7. Be willing to work on the problem,
8. Be willing to accept help from others (God's choicest blessings often go through hands that serve Him here below),
9. "Seek not to counsel the Lord, but to take counsel from His hand, for behold, ye yourselves know that He counseleth in wisdom, and in justice, and in great mercy, over all His works" (Jacob 4:10), and
10. Never give up...the Lord is there to help!

Guidance in Choosing a Husband

A Mormon girl is expected to get married and raise a family and Kathleen Horsley was no exception. She was a bit later than some in making the choice, for she had gone on a mission and was now home enjoying several boy-girl situations. Among her suitors, was her Sunday School teacher, a returned missionary named Wayne Redd. They hadn't dated much, and she hadn't known him very long. Now he had gone away for the summer, which didn't bother her too much because she was dating others.

She looked to her patriarchal blessing for advice and it said, "Pray about the man whom you will marry". She did so, obediently. Sometimes she just received a strong feeling or prompting, but she wasn't satisfied because she was not *sure*. One night she decided to ask the Lord who she would marry. She went to the Lord in faith, naming the three fellows she was presently dating, and asked which one she would marry. She was surprised at the answer, for her wise Heavenly Father knew how the situation would be resolved and told her, "You will marry none of them. You will marry Wayne."

At first she was a little taken aback. Reason reminded her that she hadn't dated him that much, that she didn't think they were very close, and certainly that she had not yet thought in terms of marrying him. But she listened to the Lord, wonderingly.

At the end of the summer, she looked at him with "new eyes" when he returned from southern Utah. Say, he *was* attractive, wasn't he? The more she looked the more he appealed to her and she was pleased that she *knew* what was going to happen, because the Lord had told her so! You might say that it even gave their romance a little boost, because the dating accelerated to the serious stage, engagement followed, and then they were married in the Salt Lake Temple. She will ever be thankful that the Lord gave her this special answer to her prayer.

You Will Have Your Heart's Desire

Brother and Sister Miles Harston were parents of a darling little boy. They were overjoyed to be parents because he brought great happiness into their lives and home! As time went on they expected other children, but no new arrivals came into their home. They would see newborn babies born to others and wish that they soon would be able to welcome a new little one into their hearts. Their son, Jerry, was not a baby any longer, but a sturdy little boy. Sister Harston wept at times because her heart ached with her unfulfilled desire to have a second little one.

One Sunday as they sat in fast meeting watching the tiny newborn infants being given a name and a blessing by proud papas or grandpas, her heart suddenly stirred painfully and tears came into her eyes as she silently prayed, "Dear Father, please let me have another child—I so much want and need a sweet little one to come into our home." The Father's answer was plain and clear and to the point, for into her mind came the words, "You will have your heart's desire."

After such an answer, patience came more easily, but time crept on and her "heart's desire" did not come. She began to explore the possibility of adoption. At last, nearly twelve years after Jerry's birth, they joyfully welcomed a beautiful baby girl into their lives in 1956. She was "born to them by adoption," Sister Harston felt, and she knew that little Jeanna was indeed their "heart's desire". As Jeanna grew and matured, her parents were so pleased and delighted with her that they never doubted that she was the Lord's answer to their prayers, for which they always remembered to give thanks.

A Voice Assured and Comforted Her

Following the death of her husband, Jane Haight was left with a family of five children still at home. Naturally, she was terribly concerned about how she was going to handle the myriad problems of child raising, family finances, and all the

other management problems which she had so strongly
depended on her husband to help resolve.

One night as she was weeping and praying for help, she
raised the poignant query, "Father, what am I going to do?"

Into the dim silence of her room a comforting sweet voice
spoke, "Do not be afraid and do not worry, everything is
going to be all right with you and your family".

What a beautiful answer she received! Peace began to
come into her mind and heart and she felt assured that her
Father in Heaven would take care of them. As the days,
months, and years moved along she knew that the help and
guidance of the Lord was continually with her. She often
went to him with her problems and received the help and
comfort she needed to raise her family and care for them.

Just Wait Until Autumn For Your Answer

A young lady who was a student at the University of
Utah at Salt Lake City in 1974 had been quietly, secretly
admiring a young man that she worked with at the Institute
of Religion. He had many fine characteristics that she
admired. He seemed to like her too, but he also seemed very
quiet and reserved. She was dating several other young men,
but not getting very interested in any of them, partly because
of her interest in that "quiet young man".

Once again she decided to pray. This time she
determined to ask the Lord if she should continue to have
hopes that her quiet young man would mean something
special in her life. Humbly she approached her Heavenly
Father, telling him of her concern for the future, and asking
him if she should continue to like this young man. As she
waited on her knees, a whole sentence came into her mind,
clear and strong, "Just wait until autumn and the answer will
come." She knew for a surety that the answer she received
was inspired and she knew that in the fall she would receive
the answer she sought.

The first day of fall quarter, the Institute was having an
opening dance which she and her girl friend discussed, trying
to decide if they should go. She was rather reluctant and
didn't think she would go, but her friend prevailed and they
went to the dance together.

As her girl friend danced off and left her, she decided to
move into the adjoining room. Just as she turned to leave, a

young man rushed up to her and asked her to dance with him. Man, what a man! They spent the rest of the evening together and had a wonderful time! How could two people find so much in common during one short evening? Well, that was only the beginning of a whirlwind courtship which ended in marriage in the Salt Lake Temple on the second day of January. She knew that God had sent her answer in the autumn, just as he had promised. She also knew that this choice was the right one because they had fasted and prayed and felt strongly assured that they were to be married. How could they help but praise God for his goodness to them?

Assistance So Temple Work Could Be Performed

Plans were laid to attend a session at the Salt Lake Temple. Four Primary officers started out happily, each laden with a suitcase of temple clothes. The four cases were locked in the trunk of the car and away they went. The trip from Bountiful to Salt Lake City was a pleasant drive for them, and they chatted lightly about their families and their church callings. When they arrived they luckily found a parking place on West Temple Street near the temple corner, a scant half block from the entrance! Things just couldn't have been better!

They climbed out of the car and locked it, going to the back of the car to get their suitcases. But dismay and alarm replaced smiling faces as the sister who owned the car tried to unlock the trunk. It would not open! Each one in turn tried to open the trunk, but the key simply refused to do the job.

Finally, one sister turned aside and begged the Lord, "Dear Father in Heaven, we are here to do endowments for four people, please help us get into the trunk and get our suitcases so we can do this work." The answer? A voice spoke within her mind saying, "Take the key off the ring and try it."

So plain was the answer, and so sure was she that the Father would help, that this sister asked for the keys. She proceeded to take the trunk key off the ring and push it into the lock. Then she turned it. The trunk door opened immediately! The four sisters gratefully thanked their Heavenly Father for his help and proceeded to the temple to do endowments for the dead.

Norma C. Larsen

Car Problems on the Freeway

Before my husband died he took complete charge of the upkeep on our family automobile, which always left me with a trouble-free car and a feeling of security. After his death, I was in constant fear of being stalled on the freeway with an ailing car and absolutely no idea of what I should do. Each time, before I could relax, I would pray that the car would take me to my destination and that I would be able to return home safely without car problems. The only trouble that occurred with the car that first year was when my two sons were driving it.

Near the end of the year, I began to receive strong feelings about my fears concerning the car. I began to think that my attitude was both foolish and immature. Yet a strong premonition kept coming that I would soon have car trouble and should be planning and preparing for it. As soon as I decided just what I would do in case of trouble, and felt calm and prepared, I knew, without a doubt, that I would shortly be tested.

One afternoon as my sister and I drove along the freeway, a spurt of water and steam flew upward from the front end of the car and it stopped running. I pulled far over to the side and my sister and I discussed what we should do. She suggested that we ask a passing motorist for a ride to the nearest telephone and call my brother-in-law to come and help us. I would have agreed that this was an excellent idea, but I hadn't prayed about it yet. When I did pray, I was told that I should just wait for a while. I could not see how that would help, but waited because I had been told to do so.

After about twenty minutes I was told to try and start the car. It started up immediately and we drove several blocks to the exit and into a handy service station where the operator found that the radiator hose had torn loose, letting the water and steam escape. Then I knew that the inspiration that we wait had been exactly the right counsel, because as soon as the motor cooled, the car started again. After the replacement of the radiator hose, we turned homeward with a feeling that help was always available and as near as a prayer.

I learned something else from that wonderful experience: although the Lord does hear and answer prayers, he also wants us to grow and mature and help solve our own problems.

Norma C. Larsen

Peaches from a Tomato Can

When I was a child, I had many miraculous answers to my prayers and through those answers my faith grew into something very precious and fine. I do truly thank my Heavenly Father for those choice testimonials that came to me in my childhood. You may think them so simple that they would not interest our Father in Heaven, but if He was mindful of a sparrow's fall, why should He not be mindful of a little child's trusting faith?

My dear mother was ill and for days was unable to eat anything. It grieved me very much because I wanted always to see her well and happy. This was a lonely Sunday and nearing time for dinner. Mother seemed a little better that day and I was so glad. I went into her room and asked her what she would like to eat.

"Well, dear," she answered, "I don't have much choice. If I eat, I will have to eat just what is on hand."

We lived about ten or twelve miles from a store, and driving a team that distance was a full day's job, sometimes taking us far into the night. We were low on groceries at this particular time. We always bought our canned goods in cases, and would sometimes purchase several cases of tomatoes, corn, etc., at a time.

At this time we did not have much of anything left in the cellar except tomatoes. Mother was so sick of tomatoes; she told me what she would rather have than anything else...if she could have it. She thought a moment, then said, "If I could really have what I want most, it would be some good cold peaches fresh from the cellar." Then she added, "I guess I'll try to imagine the tomatoes are big juicy peaches and let it go at that."

I left mother and made my way into the little bedroom where I was born, the room mother always used to go into for prayer, and knelt beside the bed. I told the Lord in my own simple way what a wonderful mother I had and how I wanted to bring her some peaches for her dinner. I arose, happy in the trusting faith—or shall I say knowledge—that my prayer would be answered. I seemed to know what to do.

I arose and hurried into the cellar and lighted a candle that I might be able to see better. There was one open case of tomatoes sitting on top of a full case. With great effort I lifted off the top box. I took the hammer lying nearby and with much lifting and banging I tore loose one board from the heavy wood case. I lifted out one can, about in the center of the case, then lifted out another can from the bottom layer. I ran like a wild child, back to the house, knowing that inside that can that I carried—with the red tomato picture on it—would be lucious yellow peaches.

When I carried a big dish of the golden fruit to her bed with some toast, she took me in her arms and wept and asked me what I did to get the peaches. I told her of my prayer and of my effort to lift the heavy case and open the other one, and how I discarded the first can and took the second one.

After I left the room Aunt Laura said, "Well, they just made a mistake when they labelled the cans. Isn't it strange it should happen just that way?"

Mother said to her, "Yes, it's pretty strange. In all my life I never found peaches in tomato cans. And that she should open another case and select a certain can; I know the Lord heard her prayers and guided her hand to that one can. And don't try to tell me differently."

I slowly pondered the situation as I went leisurely back to our prayer room and thanked my Heavenly Father for answering my prayer. Mother was up and dressed when I returned home some time later.

"Your peaches cured me, darling," she said as she hugged me to her heart.

Maggie Tolman Porter

Understanding Revealed Concerning a Baby's Death

Fearfully, but hopefully, Sister Kathleen Redd prayed to the Lord that all would go well in this pregnancy. Her constant prayer was, "Please, bless this baby that it will be born alright and that it will live." She knew that she needed the Lord's help. It was to be expected that she would be apprehensive, because this was her fifth child and she had a past record of bearing her babies early, sometimes with complications.

As she looked back on the most serious birth complication, when her second child was born, she knew that without faith and prayer and the Lord's help, her baby girl never would have made it. Although all the children had come early, Jayne's birth was the earliest—seven weeks—and she was born with a bad heart as well. But today, thank goodness, she was as sound and well as a mother could wish.

As she thought of the tiny spirit waiting to be born—the beloved little one she was carrying, she continued to pray that she would be spared another fearful experience like the one she had gone through after Jayne's birth. She begged the Lord to let her child have a more favorable chance to live.

As time moved on and she passed the crucial seven months' mark, she breathed a little easier, but her constant prayer for help was unabated. Two weeks later, as she was awakened with pains, fear clutched her heart—it was six weeks too soon! "Oh, Father, please let this little one be normal and let it live."

Her doctor told her to come to the hospital but hoped that the pains would cease. This was not to be, however, for another tiny daughter was born that morning. Within a short time the newborn infant had returned to her Father in Heaven. A heartbroken mother wept and prayerfully mourned. She pondered the situation in her mind and kept asking herself why the baby had died. She knelt in prayer and asked, "Why didn't she live when I prayed so long and hard that she would live? Please tell me, Father." In the depth of her sorrow, she heard a voice speaking to her, bringing peace and assurance with it. The words rang out clearly, "She did." Suddenly she knew that this brief moment of mortality was all of life that her beloved baby needed to experience. She could accept the Father's will.

"I'm Still in Charge..."

During a period when I was greatly distressed about the crime and evil in the world, I found myself literally walking the floor in empathy and pain for the suffering of my fellow men, especially the kind that they suffered at each other's hands. I felt I could not bear the cruelty, the greed, and self-seeking they so avariciously practice against each other. These things left me with such grief and sadness that I was praying for a way to make the world a better place to live. I knew that the gospel was the way, but wasn't there some-thing, some way, that changes could be hurried? I begged the Lord, "Isn't there something I can do to help put a stop to the evil in the world?"

Suddenly a calm voice spoke into my mind saying, "Don't forget I am still in charge of this world." At which I burst into tears and laughter, and felt an overwhelming feeling of relief as I found myself saying, "Of course you are, of course you are." Tears and laughter and relief mingled as I knew that He too was sorry about the ways of mankind, but nevertheless He was watching out for each one of us, good and bad alike, and making great attempts to reach us and help us to be our better selves. Never, since then, have I let myself reach the state of despair that I reached then, just a reminder of that calm statement, "Don't forget I am still in charge of this world." And I am once more placed on an even keel and thankful for the Lord's ever-present help.

Norma C. Larsen

Help in Repairing a Typewriter

I almost wept when the typewriter stopped working right in the middle of an important assignment I was trying to do. I was putting together a monthly newspaper for a church organization and absolutely had to get it ready immediately or it would not go out on time. "Oh, Father," I groaned, "Please don't let this happen, I just don't have time to take it to be repaired before this paper comes out. Please help me know what to do."

As I raised my head, the words came into my mind, "Turn the typewriter over and take out the screw." I immediately turned it over, took out the center screw, and the bottom came off. As I peered into the machinery, not having the vaguest idea of what to do next, the words came, "Oil there," as my glance moved over a part near the spacing bar. I hurried and got the oil and put a drop where I had been directed. This was followed by, "Turn the machine on." I reached underneath and rolled the "on" switch into position. Immediately there was a whirring noise and something revolved and threw an inch-long piece of stencil out of the lower part of the typewriter.

I exuberantly put the bottom plate back on, inserted the screw, turned the machine over and was ready to continue the job, but not without thanking the Lord once again, for His gracious help to me in a time of trouble.

Norma C. Larsen

The Spirit is in Your Yard—You Are Safe

Sister Cora Heslington had been feeling apprehensive for some time about going out into their yard after dark, especially when she was alone at home. Her fears grew until she almost hated to even take out the garbage. She would hurry out and rush right back in, feeling frightened that someone might suddenly appear and assault her or try to get into the house. She would try to reason herself out of her fears, scold herself, even offer a quick prayer for safety as she moved into the darkened yard, but she became more nervous, not less, as time went on.

One evening she had to take the garbage out, and as she started into the back yard, she silently prayed for assurance that she would be all right. She moved uneasily, still arguing with herself, "Why am I scared? This is foolish. Please help me, Father." Suddenly a calm, assuring voice came into her mind, "You don't need to be afraid in your yard and neighborhood, the same spirit that is in your house is in yours and your neighbor's yards. You are safe." She felt a warm, secure feeling permeate her being. She knew that the voice was from her Father in Heaven and she knew that He didn't want her to be afraid. As she looked about she was convinced that her neighborhood truly had a spirit of peace and love and she needn't worry ever again.

Now I Am Sure You Get Answers to Prayers

One evening in 1976 my eldest son, Clark Larsen, came to me and asked if he could talk with me privately. We went into the den, closed the door and faced each other. He has felt a conscientious concern for me and those children still at home in Bountiful, Utah ever since my husband's death and has often given me help and good suggestions. He is an especially fine man who lives close to the Lord.

He began, "Mother, you know that I haven't been able to accept that you receive answers to your prayers in words and that you are able to talk to Daddy on your wedding anniversary. You knew that, didn't you?"

"Yes, son, I did."

"Well, Mother, I decided to fast and pray and ask the Lord to help me tell you that you were mistaken and you only thought you received such answers and spoke to Daddy. I fasted and prayed and asked the Lord to help me find a way to tell you this without hurting your feelings."

I looked inquiringly into his eyes, "Yes?"

"Well, Mother, I didn't get the answer I expected," he paused and I almost held my breath, "I want you to know that I now believe—no, that I now am sure that you do get answers to your prayers in words and that you do talk with Daddy."

"Oh, Son, I am so pleased that the Lord has let you know this," I said in a burst of joy and happiness. The spirit of the Lord was rich and full in the room and I silently thanked the Father for testifying to my son.

Norma C. Larsen

Teachers Are Aided in Preparing Their Students

The school system in New Zealand is somewhat different than in the United States. As a new teacher I quickly discovered that external examinations given by the Government create a whole new set of pressures on students and teachers alike. Students who successfully pass the exams move up a grade and also receive considerable status inasmuch as the working salaries and the employment opportunities are based on successful passes. As each new grade is passed, students receive higher pay and better education allowances at the universities. Teachers whose students do well on the exams are much coveted within the school system.

In 1973, under the pressure of examinations which were just a week away, I was making a special effort to give the students all the experiences that would help them be successful. My appeals to the Lord were also that I would do what was right for the students, knowing that they had put their trust and faith in the things that I had told them.

Three days before the examination I had arrived at school early to prepare the day's review. As I walked past the storage room something told me to go back and have a look. I don't know what it was, but I remember standing there in the hall and saying to myself, "What in the world do you need to go there for?" The impression again said, "Go to the storage room." I went there, and my attention was focused on a particular piece of equipment called the Potometer. It is used for measuring the evaporation of water from leaves and stems. The thought came to me that the students should know about this instrument even though the curriculum had nothing specific about this area. I took the time to set up the apparatus and make measurements with each of the classes. I made sure that they understood the concept involved. I thought no more of the experience until after the examination.

The first student who popped into the room with a big smile on his face let me know immediately that something good had happened. Without saying anything he opened the examination booklet which they were allowed to keep. There was a drawing of a Potometer with questions about the concepts we had taught a few days previous. I know the experience was not an accident, and it humbled me to know that our prayers are answered. Our Father in Heaven accepts our intentions and desires to be a good influence and to teach correct principles.

Ronald Prows

Chapter Two

GOD ANSWERS PRAYERS THROUGH THE ACTIONS OF OTHERS

Our Heavenly Father frequently calls on others to come to our assistance to help answer our petitions to Him, or He changes conditions so our problems cease to exist or influence us. In sometimes miraculous ways our problems may be resolved or eliminated in response to our prayerful petitions and we can see that the Father contributes to their solution.

The following true accounts tell of receiving help through someone sent by God and of situations where difficult problems were removed through divine intervention.

The Man Helped Frank, Then Disappeared

I remember that day very well. It was a very hot day in 1883 at noontime. I must have been about ten at the time. The boys that were home, John and Orson, were about to sit down to the dinner that our mother was putting on the table. I noticed a worried look come to my mother's face as she placed the food before them. She asked me to say the blessing. She said she'd eat later and went outside. Her worried look troubled me, so I followed her as she crossed over to the bunkhouse bedroom, which was her retreat for prayer when she was in need. I followed a few paces behind and listened as she asked God to protect her boy, Frank, who was riding the range in Skull Valley, Utah, some twenty-five miles distant.

There were no ranches for miles and miles where Frank was working—it was out in the desert. Frank had gone after a valuable horse that had strayed away and that they feared had joined with a wild band.

31

After Mother said "Amen" she still kneeled at the bed with her head bowed, and was sobbing. I came up and put my arms about her, and asked how she knew Frank was in danger and she answered me, "The spirit of the Lord told me he was in danger, but he is all right now, dear. I know because the Lord has sent me an assurance. Let's go and eat our dinner."

That night just as the sun was setting, from my lookout on the machine shed I spotted a dust cloud rising in the distance. An hour or more later Frank walked into the house, pale and shaken. He could hardly walk.

"What happened, son?" Mother asked.

"Mother," he answered, "I was chasing the band of horses that Old Jim was with, trying to head them for home, when my horse stepped into a badger hole and keeled over. I struck my head on a rock." (Here he showed a big lump above his temple.) "I did not know anything for quite a while...."

"When was this?" my mother broke in.

"It was about noon...as clearly as I could tell."

"Yes, son, what happened next?" she eagerly inquired.

"The sun was around quite a ways," he replied. "I figured I'd be home before I was too thirsty. But the man...Mother, what was he doing out there miles from anyplace, without a horse? He gave me a drink, and brought me my horse, and lifted me onto it. I asked him if he wanted to ride with me, or where his horse was, for I could see for miles around. The band of horses I had been chasing was miles away. I could see their dust. He said he never rode a horse. I doubted his word—out there at least twenty-five miles from a habitation of any kind. I gazed about for his horse, I thought he was joking. When I turned back to ask him another question, he had disappeared. There was neither rock, tree, nor bush for him to hide in or behind. Mother, I just can't make it out."

Mother then told us the beautiful story of the Three Nephites whom Christ granted that they never taste of death, but remain upon the earth, doing good, until His second coming (3 Nephi 28). Mother said she thought that the man was, no doubt, one of those Three Nephites.

Maggie Tolman Porter

The Shoes Arrived So She Could Travel

During World War II in 1945, when shoes had to be purchased with a shoe stamp, Sister Grace Fillerup had gone to a shoe store in a nearby town. Since she would have to wait for the shoes to be ordered and mailed to her, she left her shoe stamp and the money for them. Several months later, at the end of March 1946, her beloved mother who lived in Salt Lake City passed away. She desperately needed a pair of shoes to wear for the trip from Wyoming to Salt Lake, but they had not arrived yet. She prayed that the shoes would come in time for her to wear them for the trip.

The following day, the much needed shoes arrived in the mail and she was so very thankful that she would have them to wear to Salt Lake for her mother's funeral. She told herself that our needs are not trivialities to our Father in Heaven, for this was but one among many answers she had received for her everyday problems and some of them were more unusual than others. She was so grateful that the Lord was so near and was always there when she needed help.

Someone Replaced the Brake Shoes

Diary of a prayer: Dec. 30, 1974: Prayed as usual for the Lord's help in keeping my car working safely. This seems to be one of my most scary things. I'm always afraid, as a woman alone, with a very limited knowledge of the workings of a car; I must depend on the honesty of a repairman plus the help of the Lord to keep my car working. The brakeman said the back wheel brake would need replacement, but would hold about a year.

June 1975: Brake leaking for two weeks, might not pass inspection.

August 1975: Car passed inspection.

December 1975: Brake repairman checked back brakes and said they had leaked, but were not leaking now. He turned the brakes, looked at the brake shoes, and said, "You have had the brake shoes replaced recently." I told him, "No, I have had no brake work done." He insisted, "It looks like they have been replaced no longer than a month ago. The brakes are better than the front ones. Come back for a checkup in a year." Once more I told him that I had not replaced the brake shoes. Puzzled, he answered, "Well, somebody is surely taking care of you."

I think he meant that a neighbor might have done it without my knowledge, but that is not possible. My faith in the Lord keeps growing, and I know without a shadow of a doubt that He hears and answers prayers, often in miraculous ways. I know that those brakes were not fixed by a neighbor, they could not have been, so what is the answer? When I told a lady friend about the brake shoes, and that the repairman said they were brand new, she smilingly said, "I didn't know that the Three Nephites did mechanical work." She too believed that the Lord was answering my prayers, for someone had fixed the brake shoes and how neither of us knew.

Thelma Kunz

She Wanted to Shake the Hand of President McKay

One time when my daughter, Julie, was about eight years old, we had a thrilling experience. We were then living in Tooele, Utah and had friends visiting us from Phoenix, Arizona. We were planning to take the men to the tabernacle in Salt Lake for general priesthood meeting because it was both conference and Easter the next day. That morning as Julie and I were talking she said, "Mom, do you know what I would like more than anything else in the whole world?" to which I answered, "No, tell me about it."

She answered me very soberly, "I would like to shake hands with President McKay." We were impressed with this desire of her heart and took her with us as we all went into the tabernacle that evening.

The men went inside to attend this meeting. We started to walk around to the west side of the building when we saw President McKay getting out of his limousine. He was about twenty feet away, but he looked up at us, and called to Julie to come over and shake his hand. He talked to her a few minutes, then he said, "Let me shake your hand again, you are surely a beautiful little girl." My friend and I stood back with tears in our eyes, for we knew that a miracle had happened to Julie that evening and we were so grateful for it.

Maxine Pace

The Man Was Dying for Lack of Water

It was a hot August in 1887 in Rush Valley, Utah. Mother had heard of an old gentleman who had come from Europe for the gospel's sake. He had been trying for three days to reach a friend of his youth who owned a store ten miles distant across the desert.

Early one morning mother sent one of my brothers down to the store to see if the old gentleman had arrived. The store owner did not seem concerned, but mother sent the boys out to look for him, knowing there was no water and no houses, nor any help except at our ranch.

Mother and I went in and prayed. She pleaded with the Lord that the old man's footsteps might be drawn to our home. At sundown the boys returned with no news of him.

Our cistern was about an eighth of a mile from the house, where another house had stood; the nearer cistern was empty. Mother sent Orson and me after water just as it was getting dark. There we found the poor old man, lying down, trying to reach the water. He said he smelled it, and that he had lain down to die, when a voice said to arise and go on and he would find water. He was lead to our cistern.

How happy we were to lead him to the house! The poor old man had been wandering for at least three days without water. Mother greeted him with relief and joy. She cared for him for several days as he began to slowly recuperate. She had to be careful about giving him water, for his stomach sent every drop back until she gave him warm liquids to drink. He proved to be a very wonderful Latter-day Saint. He was a temple worker, and he told us how angels had brought genealogy of his ancestors to him; how they would give the names and all data needed to have their temple work done, and he would write it down.

It seems that his friend had left the Church and this man had heard about it and wanted to save him. When he was well, mother had him taken to the store and he stayed for weeks and seemed to be doing what he desired for his friend.

Maggie Tolman Porter

The Water Was Made Sweet

Rush Valley, Utah was a wonderful county: good climate, rich soil, but—sad to say—without sufficient water for the farms under cultivation. Year after year the water situation seemed to grow worse. Our land had one of the prior water rights, but a selfish man took our water. My brothers wanted to go to the law and have it settled in a legal way, but my mother felt that going into court was a crime and she would not let my brothers take it into court. She always said, "It's better to suffer wrong than to do wrong." So our condition became very critical. We could scarcely get water down to our ranch to fill the cistern which held our drinking water, and to a pond that held water for the stock.

One year—the last year we lived there, 1887—eight weeks passed during the heat of the summer and the water was so bad in the cistern that it smelled terrible. It had a green scum on it, and had to be boiled to prevent severe illness. The pond dried up and the cattle had to go three miles for water.

My mother and I fasted and prayed, asking God to cleanse our water and make it fit for our use. Mother rose early the next morning and drew two buckets of water. It was as sweet and fresh as it had been the day it was run into the cistern. It lasted that way until we left in September of 1887 for our new home in Wyoming.

Maggie Tolman Porter

She Prayed Her Tears Would Not Spoil the Occasion

During 1974, after many months of struggling to overcome serious problems caused by colitis, Sister Helen Larsen began to see some improvement in the condition and was hopeful that the time was nearing that she might be well again. Besides faithfully following her doctor's instructions and taking the prescribed medication, she had been prayerful and had asked for the Lord's help during this time and she felt that He had helped her while she was trying to get well.

Because of this condition she had not been able to go to the temple to labor in the endowment work for the dead and yearned to go once more into the Lord's house. Did she dare? She thought, I'm well enough that I might just make it if I pray for help. Each time she approached the temple she would give an added prayer, "Please help me to make it through the session without complications, Heavenly Father." Her fear left her and while in the temple she had no further problems with her illness. She always remembered to thank the Lord for his help.

This same sister earlier, in December 1964, had an interesting experience at the temple on the occasion of her son and his wife's sealing for time and eternity. This tender-hearted sister had a history of becoming emotional on certain touching occasions and she would weep freely. Try as she would, she could not control her tears. Happy and sad occasions brought the same response until she began to feel abashed about her inability to control these tears.

The date and time arrived for the sealing and she was in fear of becoming emotional in the temple. Since she could not bear the thought of crying on this wondrous occasion, she prayed that she would be able to control the tears on that day. With full faith that she would receive help, she went to the temple to see her beloved son, wife, and children sealed and surprised them by not weeping at all. She was overjoyed and a bit amazed, and felt humbly grateful to an understanding Father in Heaven, who helps in all things!

Her Hurt and Guilt Was Drained Away

During a period of three years, from 1967-70, Sister Colleen Mirci was in the process of a divorce, trying to resolve almost insurmountable problems in her marriage. This was the eleventh time she had taken her husband back and tried to resolve their problems. Promises to work to improve the marriage were not kept, but she still questioned whether she had a right to break up her marriage and deprive her children of a father. Guilt, love for her husband, a feeling of failure and blame, all were rampant in her breast as nine months of the year she had promised him, and insisted would be absolutely final, had passed and she found her misery had increased.

For nine months she had fasted every Thursday and prayed to the Lord to help her resolve the problems and to do the right thing, until she was almost totally exhausted with trying to find the answer. She knew the fact that her husband was not a Latter-day Saint and showed little respect for her feelings about the Church caused some of the problems. Her desire to bring her children into the Church also caused friction, but worst of all was the constant verbal lashing out at her, putting the blame for all the problems on her, until she was so bowed with guilt she nearly had a nervous breakdown. At one point, the situation reached the point that she had to be hospitalized and given tranquilizers.

She decided then to take her problems to the Church for help. Spencer W. Kimball was in their southern California city visiting members of the stake and her dear friend took her to see him at a meeting. She was sitting up near the front of the hall and as Brother Kimball glanced down at her, he could see she was ill. He asked that she be taken into the Relief Society room and he came immediately and gave her a blessing.

At this time she gained enough strength to begin divorce proceedings to end the situation which had then been dragging on unresolved for nearly three years. She felt she could not take much more, so she prayed mightily to her Father in Heaven, telling him she couldn't bear it any longer. She asked him to help her lose the strong feelings of emotional attachment she had to her husband and relieve the guilt feelings so that she could obtain this very much needed divorce.

As she walked down the hall afterwards, she recalled later, she was right in the middle of the hall when suddenly it felt like someone touched her head. She stopped, as a powerful feeling of cleansing moved from the top of her head down to the tip of her toes and drained completely from her body. The power took with it the hurt, the guilt, the feeling of worthlessness, the failure, and the feeling of not being wanted or loved. A joyful feeling of self-worth, security and strength flowed into her body. She also seemed to have lost the powerful feeling of emotional attachment toward her husband and she felt free at last to make decisions which would be best for her and her children.

Thankfully she praised the Lord and took up the threads of her life. She told her husband she was leaving, that she would not wait out the remaining three months of the promised year.

With the divorce behind her, she has moved ahead to keep her children in the Church and close to the Lord. One has already fulfilled a mission for the Church and she is busily engaged in church work and trying to help others.

Chapter Three

GOD ANSWERS PRAYERS THROUGH INDIVIDUAL INSPIRATION

When you pray for inspiration to make a decision, or for help to make a right choice about something dear to your heart, or for help in selecting the right person to fill a church calling, God can give you guidance and inspiration about that which you have prayed which will help you make the proper decision. Following are true examples of situations in which God gave inspiration and guidance when He was called upon.

Choosing a Counselor

It was October 1964, Sister Mary Ostler had been chosen as president of the YWMIA and had prayerfully been seeking for two counselors. She had worked with Anna Lee Vallace in MIA before and it was easy to think of her as a counselor. She was hard working, talented, anxious to be helpful, and Sister Ostler thought, I feel she is the right one.

The choice of a second counselor was not so easy. There were so many talented sisters in the ward; so many she enjoyed working with. As she evaluated and assessed the situation, she prayed to the Lord for guidance. When she arose to her feet, she decided to ask Bishop Milton W. Russon for help. Wisely, he worked with her and made up a list of possible counselors, eliminating two or three who already were much too busy in other church assignments. At the bottom of the list he added the name of Laurel Burningham, a sister who had just moved into the ward. They knew very little about her other than she seemed to have a sweet, gentle spirit and was most helpful at all times. In short, she had very similar qualifications to the others on the list.

"Take it home, Sister Ostler, and pray about it, and I know you will make the right choice," the bishop said encouragingly.

On her knees that evening she asked for special help from the Lord in making this important decision. "Laurel's name came into my mind and it just stuck there. I was sure that she was to be the one," she later told the bishop. "But I wasn't going to say yes until I prayed again. I went to church and introduced myself to Laurel and we visited and talked for a while. That night I prayed again and the strongest impression came into my mind, that she was the one."

The bishop then said, "Just give me a day, I'll pray about it too." The next night he called her back and said, "Sister Ostler, you're right, she's the one the Lord wants." Laurel was called to serve and later Sister Ostler said, "She's just a jewel."

The Lord Wrote the Editorial

As editor of a church organization paper, I had to get the copy ready by the twentieth of the month, in order to get it printed and ready to distribute by the end of the month. Sometimes I would be so busy I would put off typing the stencil and writing the editorial until very late. In June of 1967 I really felt under pressure and prayed sincerely to the Lord, "Please help me with this editorial, I'm so late and I want it to be a good one, one that will be helpful to the members. Please help me to do it right." Confidently I arose and started to write an editorial and it literally flowed from my pen, even kept ahead of it, until I couldn't get the words down on paper fast enough. It was in my language, but I knew I had not written it because I had not worked on it, nor corrected it, nor struggled for it, but I was so grateful for this extra help and I told the Lord how I felt.

The next month I was again late starting on the editorial, but this time, I just prayed for help to do a good editorial that would contain inspirational material. Sitting before a clean sheet of paper, holding my pen in hand, I hesitated momentarily, not even searching for a subject or ideas, when the Lord spoke silently into my mind, "You thought I was going to write it for you." I burst into laughter because I suddenly realized that that was exactly what I had been doing, sitting there waiting for the words to flow as they had the month before. Well, I got to work and with the Lord's inspiration and help, I wrote the editorial. I know He helped me, but I also know He did not wish to rob me of the joy of creativity and I loved Him more dearly than ever for His wise love for me.

Norma C. Larsen

The Spirit Helped Him Accept Counsel

In June, 1970, the summer before Kevin was nineteen, he met a girl at a canyon party given by the company he worked for. He was immediately interested in her because she was vivacious and especially friendly. They began to date and had some really fun times together, which made them feel like they had been friends for a long time. They knew this was no ordinary friendship, but was very special.

They hated to be apart, so they found many opportunities to go on walks, picnics, shows, and just to sit on the front porch and talk, which helped them to see that they had much in common. Both were Latter-day Saints, and both wanted to go on missions. There was just one hitch—they seemed to be getting too emotionally involved for such a short acquaintance and they felt their friendship was progressing too rapidly towards a full-fledged romance.

One afternoon as they sat on the couch at Kevin's home, his mother was a bit disturbed because Ann put her arm around Kevin's neck as they sat talking. She did it casually, as though it was the usual thing. His mother thought, "She is too possessive. She's taking him for granted, and that worries me," but she held her peace and said nothing.

While talking to a friend, Kevin's mother was told that Ann was a "fast worker" and that she had been dating some bad characters, but his mother brushed it aside and tried not to think about it. One day she thought, "What if it is true and she is deceiving him? If he takes her at face value, it might mean the end of his plans for a mission, besides a possible marriage to the wrong girl." She decided to pray.

The answer she received from her Father in Heaven was clear and plain—he should not date Ann, she was not what she seemed. Kevin's mother was greatly disturbed by this answer and told Kevin about the answer to her prayer. He said that he felt all right about Ann, although she had told him some of the things she had done and repented of, but he would fast and pray about it.

The following Sunday he reported to his mother that he had fasted and prayed and felt it was all right to keep dating Ann, which disturbed his mother greatly. When he came home from his date with her that evening, his mother talked to him once more. Then his brother, Alvin, talked with him too and tried to encourage him to stop dating her. By this time Kevin's mother was more disturbed than ever and left the room to pray for additional help. "Oh, Father, what shall we do? He is so emotionally attached to her after only two-and-a-half weeks' acquaintance, that he can't even hear your message. Tell me what to do." She was urged to get his married brother to talk to him. Within a short time his brother came and after talking to him, Kevin said, "I don't think your situation with Kay was like mine with Ann."

At this point, Alvin, who shared the bedroom with Kevin, pulled the sheet up under his chin and began to talk to him about his responsibility to his parents. He reminded Kevin that his welfare had been uppermost with them since his birth, and that since his father was away, his mother was in charge and he should heed her counsel. As he spoke, the spirit of the Lord was so powerful in the room that all felt it and Alvin was so overcome with strong emotion that he burst into tears.

Kevin spoke up, "Alright, Mother, I'll do whatever you think I should." As he looked at her, she suggested that he cut back on his dating, but he said, "No, Mother, I will stop going out with her, but I pray the Lord will help me find a way to break off with her without hurting her," and he too wept.

The family knelt in prayer and thanked the Lord for His help in this crisis and for the comforting spirit they could feel so strongly about them in the room. There was no doubt in their minds that the problem was resolved because they had been sent the sorely needed help through the Holy Spirit.

A Fitting Memorial

Following her husband's death, Beth Gore, who lived in Bountiful, Utah felt the time had come to choose a fitting memorial for him. She wanted a headstone that would uniquely represent him. She prayed that she would be inspired to make the right choice for her husband's memorial marker. She and a friend shopped a number of places, but none that she saw seemed right to her. Her friend agreed with her saying, "They just aren't him!"

They decided to ride up around Wolf Creek, a place dearly loved by her husband. As they were driving along, suddenly a large and shapely boulder loomed before their eyes and both were inspired to know that this was the proper marker. How to get it back? They had a station wagon and with the help of their sons who were with them, they struggled and tugged and dragged the big boulder and finally placed it in the back of the station wagon. With much care they safely made the trip back to one of the dealers and asked him if it were feasible to make it into a marker.

He hesitated before saying, "Well, I've never done anything like this before, but I'd like to try it. If it doesn't split on this crack, I'll try to smooth this side."

Later he told them after working on it, "We were lucky, the crack didn't go through to the other side. It has been an interesting experience and quite a challenge."

The memorial marker stands today, beautifully embossed with an outline of the temple on it as well as the name and dates attesting to the life and death of Brother Gore. Sister Gore feels that she was inspired to choose this special marker for her beloved companion, because he always was an individualist, one who liked to make up his own mind, and she felt he would have liked it very much.

Chapter Four

GOD ANSWERS PRAYERS WITH PROTECTION AND ASSISTANCE

When we pray to our Heavenly Father for protection from harm, accident, or misfortune, He sometimes demonstrates His power so strongly that we cannot help but recognize that He has exerted His influence in our behalf. In these instances our faith is greatly strengthened. A wide variety of examples are chronicled in the following true accounts.

She Was Made Well Till Her Responsibility Was Fulfilled

While we were living in Hawaii, I was a secretary at the Hawaiian Telephone Co. and at one time was chairman and hostess for the office party. The morning of the party I was violently ill and I wondered how I would possibly put on this party for my friends. I prayed very earnestly, asking my Father in Heaven to bless me to feel better so I could make this party a success.

Almost immediately I was absolutely well and I thankfully prepared the party for the office group. We had a lovely time and I enjoyed it very much, but as the last guest departed I was back to being desperately ill again. I realized then that I had asked only to be well for the party and my prayer had been answered just as I had stated my request.

Kay Jacobsen

She Travelled in Safety

One of my single friends from the special interest group, Thelma Kunz, has a great deal of faith in the Lord. She knows

He will take care of her at all times, so she keeps very close to Him through prayer. In December, 1975, she spent a week in Logan, Utah. Before returning to Salt Lake City she had her snow tires checked so that she would feel secure on the journey home. However, as she started out one of the wheels didn't sound just right, so she returned to the service station to have it re-checked. Unfortunately the station had closed, so she stilled her fears and started out for home. As she drove she prayed that all would go well and that she would arrive safely at her destination.

She could hear a rattling noise in one wheel, the one she had been apprehensive about, and got out to check it. The hub cap was bent, so she thought it might have been responsible for the rattling and she removed it to discover that one of the nuts was missing. Prayerfully, she proceeded toward Salt Lake City and eventually arrived there safely.

The repairman she took it to the next morning shook his head in amazement and said, "It's a wonder you weren't killed on the freeway. The lug nuts are loose and two of them are gone. Besides that there are holes in the brake drum. I don't know how you made it here!" She knew that the Lord had once more protected her and preserved her life.

Protected from Flying Glass

On the afternoon of February 19, 1976, as I worked in an office in St. George, Utah, about 4:20 p.m., I was sitting about four feet from a large 6' x 6' plate glass window that was blown in on me. It previously had a small bullet hole about in the center, which may have weakened the pane somewhat. The wind had started to blow severely about 20 minutes before, with dirt blowing everywhere. I was sitting parallel to the window when it fell in, and I whirled around and put my hands up over my head, expecting to be pierced all over with the broken glass, which was about 1/4 of an inch thick. My desk has big gouges all over it, even down inside where my legs were. I shook four pieces of glass out of my hair, and down inside my clothes, but I didn't get a scratch.

Early that morning, in our family prayer, my husband had asked the Lord to especially watch over me that day as I traveled to work, and also while I was at work, that no harm would come to me. I felt the need so strongly for that help, that I reached over and patted him on the knee and later thanked him for that special prayer, telling him that I too had felt a special need for it that day. As I finished dressing, I went in and put a silk scarf around my neck and down inside my collar, something I have not done in twenty years. This prevented the glass from going down inside my clothes any more than it did.

I thanked the Lord for this special blessing and for His protecting me in the face of great danger.

Maxine Pace

Car Trouble Was Held in Abeyance

During the summer of 1960 when my grandson was just a baby and his sister, Kathy, was about 20 months old, their daddy had to go out with the Navy for six months. I flew from Hawaii to San Francisco to help my daughter, Carol, drive these darling wee ones to Salt Lake City. Our plan was to enjoy a visit with my widowed mother.

Shortly after our departure, we had car trouble and had to wait while the car was repaired. When we stopped at a gas station a few hours later, the mechanic there told us the car couldn't possibly make the trip to Salt Lake City because the repairman had not replaced a part of the motor. We prayed earnestly that we could make the trip safely and proceeded immediately. Things went well for us on the road and we found comfortable motels to rest in each evening and we were so thankful. Finally, as we reached the driveway of my mother's home, the motor suddenly stopped dead. We coasted into the driveway realizing just how blessed we had been.

Kay Jacobsen

A Miracle Was the Alternative to Death

The sun was shining and it was a beautiful day for November. Joann Green was happy because her husband had called and offered to take her out to lunch. She hummed as she dressed the three children and got their one-month-old baby girl ready to go. She thought of the wonderful life they had in this little rural town in Idaho, and of her busy and happy days spent cooking, canning, raising chickens, gardens, kids, and dogs! Yes, life was good! She glanced at the clock. It was 11:20 and if she hurried she could just make it over to her friend, Sally's, with a chicken for their Sunday dinner, then she could go on and meet her husband for lunch.

Gaiety was aglow in the children's eyes and behavior as they climbed into the car ready to set off for an adventure. The two boys were happily chattering in the back seat while her daughter and the baby were up front with their mother. She hurried along the narrow dirt and gravel road to cover the three miles to Sally's farm, keeping within the 35 MPH speed limit. Since the road was narrow and she was going up a fairly steep hill she moved over to the center of the road as she neared the top.

When the crest was surmounted she gasped in surprise and terror, for coming at her in the center of the road was a milk truck. Immediately she swung to the right onto the shoulder and down toward the steep barrow pit—her only alternative was a head-on crash. The car left the road with an almost certainty of rolling down the embankment, while she called aloud to her maker, "Dear Lord, please save us! Dear Lord, please save us!" He heard, and the car was grasped by a force which held it in perfect balance and gently drew it in a semicircle back onto the road! Incredible? Yes. The marvelous love of the Father saved this dear sister and her little family and she was in awe, but so grateful that her heart was filled with thanksgiving.

The police, later, looked at the scene and at the tire tracks in utter bewilderment. Where were the tire tracks that should have been in the barrow pit? There were none! The exit and the entry tracks were there, but no tracks in between.

That evening after all the excitement had calmed somewhat and the family was settled for the night, Sister Green was given a vision, which she later interpreted as an explanation of the alternative to that miraculous power that enfolded her car to bring it safely back to the road. She witnessed her funeral and that of her four children. She saw herself in a casket, with the wee baby laid on her breast, while alongside sat three small caskets with her beloved children in them. She heard the music, and saw the Primary chorus as they sang *I Wonder When He Comes Again*. She saw on the stand who the speakers were, noted the flowers, and felt a deep sadness.

She was to think of this experience often, to try and interpret the vision, and finally to conclude that this is what would have happened if the Lord had not intervened in her behalf; He had quite literally saved their lives. Gratitude and joy at the Lord's love and goodness to her and her family stayed with her through the years since this day in 1959 when a miracle was her only alternative to death.

Spare My Son

During World War II, Sister Romola Walker's son was part of the crew of a huge bomber in the air corps. One night while he was flying missions off the coast of China, his mother at home in Salt Lake City could not sleep. She would doze and then suddenly awaken with apprehension. This kept happening through the night. She seemed to know that her son, Raymond, was in trouble and she repeatedly went on her knees and prayed for his safety.

When she received a letter, sometime afterwards, she was told of that night and the flight of the bomber. It, indeed, was hit. Shrapnel came through and hit one of the men seated nearby. Although it came very near to him, her son was not injured.

She feels that her prayers for his safety not only aided him, but may also have prevented a more serious hit to the plane. She was full of gratitude for the Divine protection for which she had fervently prayed.

*   *   *

It has been said that "Prayer is a dialogue, not a monologue. It opens a spiritual channel between man and his immortal guide." President David O. McKay observed that "Prayer is a message of the soul. The language is not mere words, but spirit vibrations." The Master has instructed His people to, "Draw near unto me and I will draw near unto you; seek me diligently; and ye shall find me. Ask and ye shall receive, knock, and it shall be opened unto you." (D & C 88:63)

Why then, since we are encouraged to pray and contact our Father in Heaven, do we sometimes find it hard to accept and benefit from the blessing of prayer? Perhaps the following counsel from President Spencer W. Kimball might be helpful: "We know so little, our judgment is so limited. We judge the Lord often with less wisdom than does our youngest child weigh our decisions. God controls our lives, guides and blesses us, but gives us our agency." (*Ensign,* March, 1975, p. 3.) And again, "Eternal life is our goal. It can be reached only by following the path our Lord has marked out for us." (Conference Address, April 5, 1974.)

An article by President Nathan Eldon Tanner, in the March, 1975 *Ensign*, quotes President Kimball's instruction that "It is not enough just to pray. It is essential that we really speak to the Lord, having faith that he will reveal to us as parents what we need to know and do for the welfare of our families. It has been said of some men that when they prayed, a child was likely to open his eyes to see if the Lord were really there, so personal and direct was the petition."

Prayer and the many and varied answers to it is the main key to building a vital relationship with our Father in Heaven. In no other way is it possible to have such a secure, happy, protected life than by placing our hand in the Lord's, praying for help, protection, guidance, and earning it by obedience to His commandments.

Chapter Five

GOD GIVES UNSOLICITED WARNINGS AND PROMPTINGS

It almost makes one sad to contemplate that there might be some miracles given to us that we have not recognized as miracles. If we pray daily, then we may wonder how many pitfalls the Lord has helped us avoid without our perceiving the blessings we have been granted. It is truly wonderful to know that He is there, concerned always about our welfare and trying to help us.

Our problem sometimes may be that we do not recognize the "still small voice" as from the Holy Ghost. We may think it is only the product of our own over-anxious mind and dismiss or override the instruction. If, as a result of such action on our part, we have an unhappy or expensive experience, we then can come to know or recognize these spirit promptings more easily and be prepared for quicker acceptance in the future.

Some unsolicited help may be special protection or assistance which we need to save us from physical harm or help to provide us with the necessities of life. Even if we are unaware of a problem, our Heavenly Father will try to help us and guide us, and no problem is too small to warrant His attention. He is watching over us daily and knows where we are, at any given time, on our personal progression scale. Following are several examples of His help.

Unheeded Warnings Caused the Loss

Washday again! Sister Karlyn Russon sorted the clothes. She gathered up a batch, including her recently-returned missionary's levis and put them in the washer. She had picked up the soap box, when suddenly there came a clear prompting, "Go through those pockets." "Why," her mind interrupted, "he always empties his pockets before the pants go in the hamper." She was about to add the soap when again came the prompting, "Go through those pockets." Was it prudence and her own experience speaking or was it a true warning? She picked up the levis, perfunctorily patted the pocket areas and tossed them back into the washer. She added the soap and turned on the proper wash cycle.

Later she pulled the freshly-laundered clothes from the washer and piled them into the dryer. She set the timer for 'heavy load' and started to leave the room when she heard an unmistakable clicking or light thumping from the dryer. Once again, the warning voice spoke, "Open the dryer and find out what's making that noise." Disturbed, she pondered what could be the source of the clicking noise and decided it was just the studs of metal on the levis. Yes, that was it. She went about her work.

When the clothes were dry, she removed them from the dryer, piled them on the table and began to fold them. The offending pants lay before her and she impulsively started going through the pockets, to discover her son's wrist watch! Guiltily she looked back over the wash-dry period and thought of the warnings she had heard. "Why didn't I recognize them as the important warnings they were?"

She hurriedly took the watch to a local jeweler, who told her that if she had found and removed the watch before it went through the drying cycle he could have repaired it all right, but the drying cycle had beaten it so completely that it was ruined beyond repair. He added ruefully, "The water didn't hurt it. It was the dryer that did the damage."

Sister Russon felt that in future times she would recognize a warning when given to her, and act on it accordingly.

A Meal to "Feed His Sheep"

One Sunday, in Hawaii, when I began to prepare dinner, I was strongly impressed to prepare for two guests, so I anxiously prepared enough food for two extra people. I made dinner as attractive and tasty as I could, wondering all the while who my two guests would be. I was very disappointed when dinner was ready to be served and no guests had arrived, but we proceeded to eat our dinner and I got my sick husband back to bed just in time to hear the doorbell ring.

I greeted two missionaries, with, "Are you Elders hungry?" Yes they were and they were also very happy when I told them that their meal had been prepared and was waiting for them! I felt very humble and happy to have been chosen to "feed his sheep."

Kay Jacobsen

A Prompting Saves a Mother and New-Born Child

Let me relate one 'warning' that came to me by which our precious daughter Valeria's life was saved, also the life of her little son and first child, Larry.

It was a cold stormy night, about the 27th of March, 1933, and there was a blizzard on. My daughter Rhea and I had gone into the turkey business. We had borrowed a hundred dollars and purchased thirty turkey hens and were incubating more than six hundred eggs. No one ran the machines but myself.

The impression came to me that Valeria was needing me. I awoke Daddy in the middle of the night and told him. "You know, Mama," he argued, "Valeria doesn't expect to be sick for three or four weeks yet; besides you can't leave the incubators to go now."

I tried to think that it was only my worry and imagination that troubled me, and I dropped off to sleep. I awoke again in a few minutes with the feeling stronger than ever. We prayed about it and I still felt I had to go. Daddy knew of these 'hunches' or 'promptings' that I had had many times before and so he told the family early that morning that I had to go.

It was a vexed family that I bade goodbye when I rode with the mail carrier to Basin. They were sure I was doing a crazy thing to be leaving our whole turkey project to "go to the dogs," which it did; we got only twenty poults from about six hundred eggs.

When I arrived in Lovell, Wyoming, I hastened to call up Valeria and Ray and ask how Valeria was and she answered, "I'm just fine." She even came down to the station to get me. I surely felt silly and bad to have left home as I did. When

Valeria told me she felt somewhat odd, rather numb and dizzy, but fine otherwise, I asked her if she had visited the doctor regularly and was assured that she had. Only two days before she had visited the doctor, but since he was not there at the time, had left a urine sample on his desk, well labeled.

The day of my arrival was Sunday and my daughter Minnie wanted us to come to her place for dinner. Valeria did not feel too well, as she told me, but wanted to go. I told her that if she would stop and see the doctor on the way, we might as well go.

The doctor was just driving away from the old hospital. We stopped him and he and I went in to test the sample Valeria had left on his desk. When he made the test it coagulated solid...she had too much albumin. The doctor was horrified and had her come in for a fresh sample test. She did not want to bother at that time but we finally prevailed upon her to do so. The doctor found this one even worse. He called me to one side and told me that she might go into convulsions any minute. He said he would have to induce labor and take the baby to save her life. She and her husband, Ray, could not feature anything so drastic and I had quite a time convincing them to stay at the hospital for an examination. When he examined her, he opened the uterus and labor began. She was simply outraged to be forced against her will to go to bed. She never wanted to have her baby in the hospital, she wanted to be home.

There was no one in the hospital at the time, and there was no nurse on duty, but the doctor put her to bed and pains began strongly. Ray and I stayed at her bedside. In the meantime the doctor received a call from Cowley, Wyoming and had to leave. He told us he would be less than an hour and that we should just watch her. He had not been gone long, however, until she began to jerk and act unnaturally. I called the doctor's home and before he arrived she was in a convulsion. She continued to have one after another for several hours. Both Doctor Horsley and the older doctor, Dr. Croft, did everything they could for her. Dr. Horsley just cut his way in and brought the baby. In doing so he cut the baby's head and he bled until his little body was like wax.

Valeria was still having convulsions when he delivered the baby. He tossed it onto the bed without tying the cord; he said it was dead, that it could not possibly be alive with the convulsions the mother had had. I grabbed the cord to stop the bleeding and had the doctor slip a clip onto it. I carried the baby out into the hall and with the housekeeper at the hospital, Artie Willis, for my helper, and the Great Physician, our Heavenly Father, we went to work. Valeria had wanted that precious baby for ten long years and I knew if the Lord saw fit to let her live, she could not stand it if her baby was gone.

I asked Artie to get a pan of warm water and one of cold water. I gave the child artificial respiration by blowing into his mouth until his lungs were distended, then releasing the air by pressure. I had Artie time me—eighteen times per minute. Then I would place the baby first into the warm water, then into the cold. After more than a half hour I saw signs of life, and ere long there was a weak cry from him.

I shall never forget how Dr. Horsley looked when he stepped out where I could see him. He was covered with blood and tears were streaming down his cheeks. He said that as great a miracle had happened as he had ever read about.

I tried to telephone Daddy to come. We had no phone and Basin, Wyoming, could get no one up as it was about 1:00 o'clock in the morning. I told central to ring everybody on the line until someone answered. I told him how things were and he went and brought Daddy. Valeria was about gone. She knew no one and continued having one convulsion after another. She did not even know that she had a baby.

Daddy arrived about sunrise. He brought Brother Tippetts with him. Brother Tippetts had been delivering milk. He was a counselor to Brother Croft in the stake presidency, so Brother Crofts, Brother Tippetts, and Daddy administered to her.

Daddy was indeed God's mouthpiece. He promised her life and health and strength, and that she would live to raise her family. She never had another convulsion. Daddy simply called her out of her coma. She saw her little son and was very happy.

If I had not heeded those promptings, she would not have lived, or the child either. It was indeed a marvelous thing. I never took time to kneel to pray, I prayed aloud to my Heavenly Father as I worked over the baby. I felt it would take *faith* and *works*, and showed my faith by my works in that case.

Maggie Tolman Porter

He Failed to Heed the Warning

When World War II was in full swing, young men were being drafted to serve in Europe and the islands of the Pacific. Vital commodities were rationed, and gas, meat, sugar, and even some clothing were very scarce. Every family carefully apportioned out coupons for gas, to use only where most needed, with pitifully little going for recreation.

Four young men from Salt Lake City, Utah, all buddies, had received draft notices. The four had accepted them with mixed feelings as they prepared themselves to go and serve their country. "Let's have a big day before we go—let's splurge our gas coupons, and go on a picnic and an outing," one of them suggested. They all agreed, so the planning got underway. The day was chosen, the place was selected, and dates with young ladies were made. They pooled their hoarded gas coupons and joyfully looked forward to having a really special day to remember.

As the day drew near, one of the young men, Henry Bredthauer, was filled with strong prompting that he should not go. But, why? As the feeling persisted, he spoke of it to his mother and she said, "I, too, have a strong impression that you should not go, but I hated to mention it, but if *you* have it also, maybe you'd better change your plans.

When Henry told his buddies that he strongly felt that they shouldn't go, they argued that there wasn't a reason in the world for not going and outvoted him on any of his suggestions to change their plans. Against his better judgment, and still feeling some apprehension, he set out. Gradually, as they headed toward Logan Canyon, he relaxed and began to enjoy himself.

He and his date were in the last of the three cars. They weren't going very fast, between 30-35 MPH, when they approached a curve. As he turned the steering wheel to negotiate the curve, the steering apparatus suddenly failed to respond! The car ploughed head-on into the hillside, smashing and ripping the chassis. The young lady with him was hurled through the windshield head-first, and received a long and circular gash from the left side of her mouth across and down her chin on the right side and back toward the center of her neck. Aghast at the sight of her face laid open this way, he spontaneously reached across her and by placing his hand beneath the wound pushed the flesh back in place over her jaw.

Directly behind them, and witnessing the accident, was a doctor who stopped his car and hastened to give help to the couple. He told the young man, "Just keep your hand right there where you have it and come with me to the hospital in Logan." They got into his car and proceeded to the hospital where four hours were spent in surgical repair work on her face. Henry then had to call the young lady's parents to sorrowfully report the outcome of the accident. He was filled with remorse because he had not heeded the warning that had been given to him. He was certain that the next time he would accept such promptings and act on them.

She Suddenly Knew It Wasn't a Tumor

Mrs. H. had been having trouble with her back for some time and her doctor believed she would probably have to have a spinal fusion. He recommended to her that she go to the Mayo Clinic for further tests and a second diagnosis. With some apprehension, but with a strong feeling of assurance also, she took a plane to Minnesota, leaving her children in her husband's care and was soon admitted to St. Mary's Hospital, one of the two served by the Mayo Clinic.

Following a number of tests, the doctors frankly told her that her spine problem was probably coming from a brain tumor and further tests were to be performed the following week. The latter part of the week, she was told that she would need a pneumo-encephalograph, for they suspected a tumor at the base of the brain, and if they performed this test to locate the tumor, it might be disturbed and need immediate removal, so they requested that her husband be contacted and asked to come and be with her. Both a neural specialist and a neuro-surgeon came in and told her that they were almost sure that she had a tumor in the base of the brain, and cautioned her that she might not come through the operation, or she might sustain severe brain damage.

On Friday, she contacted her husband at their home in Virginia and told him the diagnosis results and they made plans for him to come to her on Sunday as the tests were scheduled for the following Monday. He arrived at her bedside with a sad but supportive attitude which she gratefully accepted. Tension had been increasing in her until she felt extremely nervous.

They left her room, that Sunday afternoon, and walked down the hall to the small chapel, feeling a strong need for

comfort from the Lord. As they entered the chapel, they
noted it was very dim in there. They could just see a figure up
near the front and also thought they saw someone near the
back of the room, but did not turn to look. With his arm
around her, they moved down the aisle toward the front and
when they were seated she suddenly began to cry, and once
started, the tears flowed more rapidly until she was sobbing
almost out of control. Suddenly there came, simultaneously, a
brightening of the room, almost as though a light had been
turned on, and her tears were replaced with a strong and
secure knowledge, or prompting, that she would be all right.

She turned to her husband and said in a decisive voice,
"I'm just fine. I do not have a brain tumor," and as he
protested, she added, "Don't worry, no matter what they
think, I don't have a brain tumor." Yes, she *knew* and she no
longer was desperately frightened as she had been earlier, so
she helped her husband overcome his surprise and fears, by
her continuing attitude of complete assurance. She knew that
she had been given a very special blessing and a reassurance
when she needed it so badly. Later, when she underwent an
operation on her spine which included a fusion, she accepted
it easily and made very good progress afterwards. In
addition, she was delighted that they found no cancer
present. She still looks back on this experience as a most
special spiritual experience and holds it very sacred.

He Had Time to Leap to Safety

In September, 1887 our family moved from Rush Valley,
Utah to Star Valley, Wyoming. As my 20-year-old brother
Frank was driving one of the wagons loaded with household
goods up through Logan Canyon, he could see a narrow
dugway a few hundred feet ahead. Approaching him were
four or five loaded wagons hauling lumber. He had the upper
side, which was his right, but the men demanded that he pull
onto the lower side next to the river. He refused. They had
words, as he was only a boy alone with the outfit. They
demanded he pull down. He left his outfit standing on the
upper side and ran back to camp for his rifle. He was not
going to move his team. Mother would not let him take the
rifle. While they were arguing over it, the teams of the
lumber wagons drove by. They had moved Frank's outfit
down on the lower side and had left it standing, with the bank
crumbling away under the hind wheels.

When Frank returned he could see the danger his outfit was in. A man drove up and tried to help him. He removed the lead team and was on the lower side, driving. When he spoke to the horses they began to move the wagon. Suddenly the whole bank caved away! Instead of immediately falling, the wagon seemed to hang in mid-air until he was able to jump to safety, then it tumbled into the river, landing upside-down with all of our precious furniture and dishes. The only thing that we were able to rescue unharmed was mother's new Singer sewing machine which had been taken to pieces and packed in a box for the trip and although the box broke, scattering the pieces, Frank rescued them and mother dried and oiled them and later assembled them in Wyoming.

We knew that the Lord's help in delaying the fall of the wagon had saved Frank's life at this time.

Maggie Tolman Porter

Prompted to Avoid the Yellowstone Earthquake

For weeks the family of Bishop Milton W. Russon had been planning their vacation. The itinerary was completed after much discussion of what was most important to see, and all was in readiness for the big vacation this summer of 1961! They had made a copy of their daily schedule with overnight stops listed, their daily route and all the pertinent details so his business partners would know where to reach him at all times. Soon they'd be on their way to Yellowstone Park!

With a scant five days to go before the big takeoff, the excited family were startled and surprised when Bishop Russon came home from work that night and said, "I think we ought to go to Denver for our vacation." That was a shock, but after some discussion the family went along with the new plans, which included making up a new itinerary. It wasn't such a strange request to make, after all, because they had many friends to visit in Denver, having been stationed there while Bishop Russon was in the service in World War II. There were but three of them at that time, mother, dad, and a little son. They became more enthusiastic about the trip as they discussed it and Bishop Russon admitted that the idea for the change just "seemed" to be the right thing to do because feelings were coming to him that Yellowstone was *not* the place to go.

During the trip they received the sad news about an earthquake disaster at Yellowstone Park, where many people were killed by earth slides during the upheaval. They were thankful that they had not been in Yellowstone at that time, because they too might have been seriously injured or killed as so many others were.

Upon arriving home, Bishop Russon's prompting, or as he knew later, his "warning" was inspired and had indeed saved their lives. Checking with their original itinerary, it showed that they would have been at the exact place and time of the very worst disaster, with a high probability that they would all have been killed.

They then knew that their last-minute change of plans was inspired in order that their lives might be saved.

Years later Bishop Russon became a mission president. Following his return to Zion he was made a stake president. The Lord no doubt spared their lives, that they might serve others and they have always continued to do so.

A Soldier Prepared for the Battle

During the Korean conflict, Miles Harston was decorated with the Silver Star for gallantry in action. It was a true miracle that he survived the war—his faith and a prompting, plus the Lord's guiding hand, brought him through.

During the early days of the Korean conflict, Brother Harston was home in Wyoming on furlough, hoping that his Guard unit would not be sent into battle. As he waited for his orders he and his wife visited with a beloved Aunt, Maggie Porter, who throughout her life had received many promptings which she had accepted as guidance from the Lord. She had a message for Brother Harston which she hesitantly gave to him, "I feel prompted to tell you that you will be in great danger, with bullets flying around your head. You'll be in the midst of a terrible battle. However, you will come through all right! You must have faith that the Lord will take care of you and both you and your wife must live your religion and keep the Lord's commandments."

When he was sent into battle, Aunt Maggie prayed fervently for him, always worried because she had told him of her promptings and afraid that it had not been wise to tell him. Later she found that her prompting had brought great comfort to him at the front, for he knew that he would return home despite the injuries which he received. Prayerfully he thanked the Lord for this knowledge and comfort.

Her prompting proved accurate, for he found himself on the battle front in a virtual "pocket" where they could not turn or retreat when a huge wave of Chinese soldiers advanced and gave battle. The casualties were devastating and the bullets were literally whizzing around his head. Then he remembered Aunt Maggie's words and knew that he would come through all right. He always remembered to thank his Heavenly Father for his help and because he was not seriously wounded or killed.

Your Daughter Will Have an Accident

One evening in the spring of 1976, Harold Donaldson began to have a strong prompting which he believed was from the Holy Spirit. It was clear: "If you let your daughter take the car this evening, she will have an accident." This alarmed him considerably. He asked himself, "Are you sure this is from the Lord, or are you just feeling apprehensive for another reason?"

The feelings were growing and the assurances increased. When his daughter, a short time later, asked him if she could take the car to run a necessary errand, he told her, "No." The young lady was not satisfied with the answer, as it seemed to her that the errand was more important and necessary than his alleged prompting, which seemed more like the usual parental anxiety. Thusly she importuned him to take the car, assuring him that no accident would happen, because she would be especially careful. She was confident that all would be well and that there was no cause for alarm.

How hard it is to be sure, he thought, and how hard to say no, so as she persisted, he finally gave her permission to take the car, but the apprehension would not leave him after she drove off.

As she arrived home later, he greeted her at the door with anxiety, "How bad was the accident?" he queried.

"Well, I didn't total the car." she replied, "But I did have an accident."

How difficult to always *know* when the voice of the Lord speaks. How hard to differentiate, at times, between a true warning and our own over-anxious mind's voice! In time, prayerfully, we will recognize and stand firm for a true warning.

His Unexplained Return Saved a Life

In 1941, sixteen-year-old David Donaldson was emptying the trash at the mill in Ogden, Utah where he worked. It was just a routine job for him. Rising in the open shaft, the doorless freight elevator approached the floor. He wheeled the cart across the metal plate and jumped onto the floor of the elevator as it continued to rise. The cart had not quite cleared the plate, so he bent forward to pull it completely on. As he bent forward he suddenly slipped and fell head-forward, sliding partially into the elevator shaft. As the elevator continued its ascent, he was scraped between the cage and the wall. He screamed in agony as it moved upward. "Please help me, Lord," he begged.

It was just after 6 p.m. and everybody had left the mill. Miraculously, one man was prompted to go back, and as he entered the building he heard David's screams and rushed to turn off the elevator. If he had not returned just at the time he did, the metal plate on the floor above most certainly would have severed David's body as he lay pinned between the shaft and the cage. A blow-torch was required for them to rescue David, whose clothes were completely torn from his bruised and scratched body.

Later, the man who saved his life said that he hadn't worked that late in years and normally would have been gone by six o'clock. He didn't know why he had such a strong prompting to return to the building until he saw David's predicament, then he knew that God meant for him to return to save David's life.

Prompted to Pray as the Pilot Bailed Out

Henry Bredthauer and three high school buddies had all been inducted into the service in the fall of 1943. One had become a pilot, two others were in the infantry. These three had already gone overseas in the spring of 1944. Henry was in basic training at Fresno, California and was lying in his bunk one evening when he received a strong prompting to get out of bed and pray. But what for? He was bewildered, but the prompting was strong. Then he saw a man's face, indistinct, the features clear, and heard a voice saying, "Pray for me or I'll die." He tried to discern which of his three buddies it might be. As he gazed at the face, he realized it was Joe, who was a pilot in the air force.

Henry thought, "I must be imagining this," but the strong feelings persisted and he said to himself, "Joe must be in trouble." He climbed out of the bunk and began a fervent prayer that Joe's life might be spared. Such strong promptings absolutely could not be ignored for long, he knew that his prayer was urgently needed.

Later he learned that at the time that he had the strong prompting to pray, Joe was bailing out of his plane after it took a direct hit, and he probably would have died in the return to earth if Henry had not been prompted to pray and had followed through with that prayer. As it was, Joe's life was spared, and he lived to thank Henry for that prayer. Henry, too, is very thankful that he received the prompting which also proved to be a valuable lesson in obedience.

Alerted to Danger by a Voice in the Night

One wintry night in 1956, Bishop Milton W. Russon of Bountiful, Utah, awakened his wife saying, "Honey, my father is outside. He just called me like he always does. I heard him say, 'Milt, Oh, Milt!' loud and clear." Struggling out of a deep sleep she comforted him, "You probably just dreamed it dear." and turned over and went back to sleep. She barely heard his affirmation that "I'm sure I heard him."

Bishop Russon was awake enough by then to feel very puzzled. Yet, he thought, when you are awakened like that you can get confused. He was unable to settle down again. A growing awareness or urgency of some kind left him unsettled, so he decided to go and look outside. He pulled his robe on, stepped into his slippers, and made his way toward the back door through the kitchen, where he immediately detected a strong odor of gas. Alarmed, he started to look for the problem. The furnace light had gone off and gas was rapidly escaping. He soon remedied this by turning the main valve off and immediately opening all doors and windows in the kitchen area to let the gas escape.

Later he was able to start the furnace again and close the doors and windows. He knew then, without a doubt, that he had heard the call, "Milt, Oh, Milt" in order to awaken him so he could discover the peril his family was in. The family feels that they probably would have perished in the night if he hadn't been aroused to the danger, and they are so thankful to the Lord for once more preserving their family.

His Mother-In-Law Knew of His Peril

During the Korean War, Brother Miles Harston, a National Guard recruit from Lovell, Wyoming, was involved in a terrible battle where the troops were trapped in a 'pocket' and waves of Chinese soldiers pushed ahead and engaged them in combat. It later turned out that as the battle was being waged, Brother Harston's mother-in-law, who was visiting relatives in Utah, was awakened in the night and apprehensively said, "Miles is hurt." She paused and was prompted to add, "Oh, no, he's all right." She was aware that she had been given a warning of the serious plight that he was in, but hesitated to tell her daughter. Instead she asked her if she had heard from her husband. Sister Harston said, "No, I haven't," and then wondered why her mother asked her this same question again within the hour.

Her mother did not tell her of her warning. "No need to alarm her," she thought. However, Sister Harston did feel apprehensive too and when they returned to Wyoming she called a friend whose husband was in the same Field Artillery company as her own husband and asked if she had heard from him. She was told that her friend had received a letter from her husband which told of the terrible battle that Brother Harston had been in, but stated that he was all right.

When Sister Harston told her mother the news about her husband, she was then told of her mother's warning experience in the night, the very night of that same devastating battle.

His Mother Was Aware of His Illness

A woman's heart never rests easy when a son or husband is away at war. So it was with Sister Mamie Donaldson of Ogden, Utah, when her son, David, was in action during World War II in no-man's-land between Belgium and Germany. His infantry troupe piled up a 45% loss, and his company had but 12 men left after those fearsome battles. November 18, 1944, Sister Donaldson was awakened by a voice calling, "Mother!" which she took to be the voice of her daughter who was recuperating from pneumonia. "Are you all right, dear?" the mother questioned. When she found it was not this daughter who had called, she questioned the other children and received the same answer.

Then she knew that the voice that had called her must be her beloved son who was away in Europe. She was fearful that he had been injured in battle and prayed that his life would be spared. When the letter came, she found that he had been badly injured on that fateful night in November, for as he was following a soldier who had stepped on a mine, he too suffered severe damage to both of his legs. He had managed to crawl into a ditch and was rescued by the medics. The injury was so severe that it was thought that at least one of his legs would have to be removed. He had been moved to England where a heroic effort was made to save his legs which by then had gangrene.

On Christmas Day, Sister Donaldson kept receiving impressions that her son was terribly ill until she feared for his life. It was a sad Christmas day for the family, for all were very concerned about their beloved brother and son. The mother wept and prayed for David throughout the day.

When he came home with 100% disability, he related to her his experiences in England. He told his mother that he had almost died on Christmas Day and said, "It would have been so easy to have died, the only thing that held me back was the thought that my mother's heart would break if I didn't come back. I knew she was praying for me and I knew that I must not give up." So he came back and received a mighty welcome from his family who had waited so fearfully and prayerfully for him while he was away. When they knew he was coming home they thanked the Lord that his life was spared to return him to his family.

A Childhood Prompting—He Would Marry an Irish Girl

One day in December 1959, Brother Dermont Larsen was riding along 3rd West street in Salt Lake City, Utah when it was suddenly made known to him that he was now the grandfather of a blue-eyed blond baby girl! It was his first grandchild and he felt very pleased and elated. He hurried back to the store where he worked and called home. His sweet wife was so excited when he called, she said, I just heard from Brent—Dar had a baby girl, she's blond and blue-eyed like her daddy. Brent says she's a little beauty like her mom." Brother Larsen smilingly told her, "I was just calling you to tell you that I already knew about the baby!"

"How come?" she replied.

"Well, as I was riding along, the inspiration just came across to me and I was aware that she was born." They checked the time and it was at the time the baby was born that he had received this precious knowledge.

He was able to accept this blessing easily because once before in his very early years he had received just such a manifestation, which also turned out to be right! One day he had suddenly been given the knowledge that the girl he would marry would be a brown-haired, but blue-eyed Irish girl. He had treasured this knowledge to his heart all his growing-up years. When he was in high school, he met a cute and saucy young lady, whose name definitely was not Irish, but since he was so entranced by her sweetness and her fun personality, he kept dating her. In time he found out that her father had died while she was very young and she had taken the name of her stepfather. Her 'true' Irish name, Helen Dougherty, did not make him love her more, but it certainly verified the special knowledge he had been given as a young boy. He did not tell her about his secret until after they were married in 1933, but through long years of an especially happy marriage they both knew that it was meant to be.

A Son Dies When a Father's Prompting Goes Unheeded

Two of Brother Marion Hammond's young sons planned to take their nephew from California out to hunt rabbits. He was visiting with them on their farm, located west of St. Anthony, Idaho. As they prepared to go, Brother Hammond received a strong prompting that if they went one of them would be seriously injured, so he told them they ought not to go. They tried to allay his fears by telling him of all the safety measures they would take. He told them that he was certain that one of them would get hurt, but they would not be stayed. They reminded him that rabbit hunting was one of the pleasures the boy had looked forward to when he came to visit, and that he had even brought his own gun.

When the father could see they could not be dissuaded, he sent their older sister along to guide and direct them. She drove the car to an open field and sat watching them as they spread out and began walking across the snow-covered field. In less than five minutes, Steven, who was not much more than 13-years-old, suddenly fell forward onto the snow. The other boys caught up to him and said, "Come on, Steven, quit clowning and get up!" When they received no response from him, they turned him over to find a wound in his head. Although they looked carefully to see the source of the bullet that had wounded him, they could find no one. He was taken, unconscious, to the LDS Hospital in Salt Lake, but never regained consciousness and soon passed away.

How many lives would have been changed if Brother Hammond could have persuaded them to heed the warning he had received?

Chapter Six

GOD PROTECTS AGAINST EVIL SPIRITS

At some time in our lives we may have an unhappy experience with an evil spirit which we attribute to any of several causes. We may innocently have been struggling to gain a testimony of the gospel, or we may have entertained strong doubts about the existence of a God. We might have been lax in keeping the commandments, although converted to them, or some unknown purpose of the Lord might have been served.

It is possible that the Lord permits this experience to occur so that we might know that staying within the circle of his loving care is a happier way of life. It is true that Satan tempts us many times in our lives, but the appearance of an evil spirit is a special kind of testing for which God provides us with the means to withstand—we have the gospel and the priesthood.

The following true experiences illustrate how calling on the Lord in sincerity, or receiving a blessing from the priesthood helps us vanquish the evil spirits who may be trying to overcome us.

They Felt Fear as an Evil Spirit Entered

Trudy, a brown eyed seventeen-year-old had been talking, as many times before, to her best friend, Ann, about her problem in believing in the existence of God. Although her mother was an active Latter-day Saint, her father was not, and Trudy shared some of his doubts about religion and God. She and Ann attended seminary and at times stayed after their class to discuss their questions with the teacher. It was an important subject with them.

One Saturday afternoon in the spring of 1958 as they lay on the double bed in Trudy's room, in her home in Salt Lake City, Utah they returned once again to the same subject. "Is there a God?" Trudy voiced the question as she lay on her stomach on the big bed, turning to look at Ann as she thoughtfully looked at the ceiling. Then what was it she said? "Why is it so important to think there is a God, when so many people get along nicely without one?"

Ann was about to answer when her horrified gaze came to rest on one of the small windows in the white basement bedroom and she watched a black smoke-like figure enter the room and hover in the air. She was terribly frightened, but more, she felt an oppressive, evil aura in the room as well! Her voice stuck in her throat and Trudy, who had not seen it, whispered, "Oh, Ann, I'm so scared."

"So am I," choked Ann fearfully. "Let's pray."

The two girls got on their knees and prayed fervently that the Lord would take away this evil spirit with its oppressive air.

The black figure moved across the room and dropped down to touch Trudy on the back. As they prayed pleadingly to the Lord, "Dear Father in Heaven, please take away this awful thing." they felt, then saw, the spirit move up and over to the window and disappear.

A release of tension and fear and thanksgiving so touched their hearts and feelings at that time that Trudy spoke for both of them when she said, "I'll never again doubt that there is a God."

Conflict with Evil While Seeking a Testimony

August 12, 1966 was a Friday that I shall never forget, for it was on this day that I received my strong, burning testimony of The Church of Jesus Christ of Latter-day Saints. The events leading up to this treasure will always be considered as a reminder of the power and truth of the church.

The experience started after I had finished writing to Kolene Russon about the happenings of the day before and about our friends here in Bountiful, Utah. It was about midnight when I finished writing and got ready for bed. I got down on my knees to say my prayers, including in it the desire to know beyond a shadow of a doubt that The Church of Jesus Christ of Latter-day Saints was the only true church upon the face of the earth. I had been asking this for some time now, but tonight seemed different.

Feeling a warm, but not yet burning sensation, I crawled into bed, still wondering about what I had just asked about. "If others could receive the Lord's help in answer to that question why should I, too, not receive help?" I wanted to find out for myself if it were true so I began to pray more strongly and more humbly for a testimony. I also wanted to know for a surety that Joseph Smith, David O. McKay, and the prophets of old, Isaac, Abraham, Jacob, Moses and others were true prophets.

A tremendous feeling entered my body and seemed to grow more intense. Suddenly a thought crossed my mind, would this same feeling come if I asked if the Catholic Church were true? I had no sooner thought about this when a strange, but terrible feeling of evil came into my clasped hands and started up my arms. It continued spreading until my whole body was possessed by this strange force. I have never felt anything like it, but it resembled the sensation of something trembling deep within me, such as you would feel after being terribly scared. This force acted upon my muscles so as to contract them into knots and roll me into a ball. Fighting it off with what faith I had and with the help of my Father in Heaven, I could keep it from overcoming my body.

Again I asked the Lord for a burning testimony of the church, knowing that all other churches were not his church. In my prayer, I expressed my desire to have my testimony come through my faith, knowing that it is better to believe by faith alone than to have a manifestation. Little did I know that through this very thing I was to receive my treasure this very day.

Still feeling the evil spirit inside me, I laid in bed, still praying silently for my testimony. I began to toss and turn and cry, continually feeling the contraction of my muscles. I was weakening at a tremendous rate of speed—so fast that I began to sweat. Then, almost instantly, I was cold—freezing cold. I continued to call upon God, asking him to be relieved of this torment that I might have a good night sleep and always asking for a burning testimony.

When the trembling sensation quieted some, I cried myself to sleep. Almost immediately I was once again possessed by the evil spirit which hit harder this time, adding to the agony a shrill-sounding whistling noise. I again called for God's help and through my faith I quieted down enough to go back to sleep. I slept for about 10 minutes, then I was again awakened by the evil influence. This time he came close to conquering me, for I awoke spinning around at a tremendous rate of speed. I was also engulfed in fire and surrounded by evil spirits. With all my strength I, for the last time, called upon the Lord for help that I might be delivered from this force. I soon stopped spinning and saw the spirits and fire leave the room. I was shaking badly and completely worn out.

At this point I realized that the only way to get relief from the devil was to have my Dad place his hands upon my head and through the power of the priesthood and through my faith, cast the devil out. I decided to go to him, so I started up the stairs. Again I began to shake and cry vigorously as if to wear me out before I could reach my Dad. I had to pull myself up by the handrail in order to reach the top. I then went into my Dad's room where he was asleep. My little sister, Marilyn, had climbed into bed with him because Mom and Marci were away at camp. When I tried to tell him what was wrong and that I needed help, I could not. The evil influence caused me to shake and cry so badly that all I could do was to lay there and sob. It took about 30 seconds to regain enough strength to tell him that I had been fighting the devil and needed the power of the priesthood to cast it out. I then fell on the bed thoroughly exhausted.

Lying there, I gained enough strength to walk out and sit on one of the kitchen chairs. My Dad, placed his hands on my head and through the Holy Priesthood which he held, commanded the evil spirit to leave my body. Instantly, I stopped shaking and sobbing and slowly felt the spirit leaving my body. In his prayer, Dad asked that I might receive a strong testimony of the church, also that I might live a good, clean life and accomplish my goals. As the prayer ended, the last of the evil influence left my body and was replaced by a strong, burning testimony of the church.

After thanking my Father in Heaven I went to bed to fall asleep, plain exhausted and knowing that the devil was gone for the night. Later my Dad told me that during his prayer he had heard someone going up my sister's stairs and when he finished he expected to see my sister, Taunie, standing there. Instead he saw a large flash of light, but heard no accompanying sound. My little sister, Marilyn, who by this time was almost petrified with fear, also heard the steps and saw the flash, but noted that there was not a cloud in the sky. They had gone to check Taunie, but found everything all right with her and decided that the flash of light they had seen might have been the evil spirit leaving the earth for the night.

Kenneth Dail Webb

The Evil Spirit Caused Him to Observe the Sabbath

A few months before our eldest son was to reach the age of 12 and to be given the Aaronic Priesthood, my husband had an experience which changed the course of his life. He had come home to Salt Lake City from World War II determined to continue active in the church and not to let anything interfere with that promise to himself. However the pressure of getting a new business started was soon upon him. Even with long, long, daily working hours he soon began to feel that if he was to get ahead in business, he would have to work on Sundays again. He had the goal of retiring early and working full time on church and civic activities, and to hasten that goal he felt he had to work on Sundays.

The 14th of May, 1954, I was in the hospital at the birth of our seventh child when my husband awakened from a sound sleep one night to see, standing at the foot of the bed, a black smoke-like apparition. There was a most oppressive feeling in the air. Fear stirred in his breast as it rose, hovered over him, and almost seemed to overpower him. He struggled to breathe and fight it off and prayed for help from his Father in Heaven. After a few minutes of struggling and praying he felt strongly impressed to cast it out by the power of the priesthood and he did so, in the name of Jesus Christ. The evil spirit immediately left the room.

Exhausted and sleepless, he prayed and asked the Lord for an explanation of the intruder. He felt, then, that it was a warning that he should be an example to his son by participating in the priesthood meetings regularly once more. He was a very conscientious Father and dearly loved his children. He felt that this was surely the right thing to do, so willingly he began keeping the Sabbath holy again. I remember him saying, "When I was working on Sunday, I thought I *had to*, but when I stopped working on the Sabbath, I knew that I didn't *have to*." Never again did he let work interfere with his church participation, unless for an exceptionally heavy and temporary work load.

Norma C. Larsen

Interference with Their Temple Labors

Brother and Sister Les Bryant and a group from the Denver, Colorado area, were on their way to the Salt Lake Temple to do endowments and sealings. Sister Bryant was a convert to the church and she and her husband had been married for a short two years. Each had brought into their union a young daughter by a previous marriage. They had been to the temple but once, when they were married and sealed for time and eternity, so they were looking forward happily to renewing their temple covenants as they did endowment work for some of her departed ancestors. The group they were flying with, early in 1964, was composed of married couples and some who had completed Project Temple and were bringing their children to be sealed to them as they completed their marriage vows for time and eternity.

They were a happy, bustling group who arrived at the temple and moved along through registration and on into the dressing rooms. For some strange reason Sister Bryant seemed to have an awful struggle getting ready. Why, it was inconceivable all of the things that went wrong: her slip went on backwards, her dress would not slide down properly, and her stockings were inside out. She commented to herself, "Is it because I am nervous? But I don't feel nervous, just very annoyed." She checked the packet of clothes she was to carry and the sash was missing. As she was about to go and get another one she discovered the sash under the small seat in the dressing alcove that she occupied. Her frustration mounted, but she tried to keep calm and finally joined the other sisters in the ante-room. She almost felt like crying because she did not have the sweet happy feeling she had had on the plane at the anticipation of returning to the temple. She just could not understand it.

As she waited her turn in the next-to-last room, when the group slowly moved into the last room, someone whispered in her left ear, "This is the silliest thing I've ever seen." but it was obvious that the words were not spoken by the lady next to her, so where did that voice come from? She felt alarmed and unhappy.

Later, in the waiting room she met Brother Bryant and was astounded to find that he had experienced very much the same problems. It was as though someone was interfering with his attempts to get dressed—he even lost his name tag and very nearly missed out on the entire session (or so he thought). They almost wished they had not come.

They spoke to their Stake President about it and told him how miserable they felt and how they sensed that something was trying to keep them from completing the work. He was simply amazed, and could hardly believe it, because he had such a wonderful experience that day. Could it be possible that an evil spirit could enter the temple? They had no other answer. It was as though Satan did not want that family temple work completed and had tried to thwart the Lord's work. They had almost a fear of returning to the temple, afraid that they might repeat the experience.

Within two years they moved to the Salt Lake area and wanted to go to the temple and do her family's work, but an aversion persisted for some time until they finally made a strong fight against it and went to the Lord in prayer. At last they went to the temple and completed the endowments on her family records. Later Brother Bryant became a set-apart temple worker and the earlier experience faded from their minds, no more to return.

A Pre-Mission Struggle

When Brother Porter was about 23 years old, in 1892, he was called to fill a mission to the Central States Mission. It seemed that almost everything he tried to do toward filling the mission miscarried. At last the day came for him to go to the Logan, Utah, Temple for his special ordinances before leaving. He borrowed his uncle's fine riding horse to ride through the mountains to Logan, before he could leave on his mission. The horse was a fine sure-footed animal, never known to stumble, but the horse fell on his leg and almost broke it. He managed to remount the animal after the fall and rode on toward his destination.

The pain was most severe in his swollen knee and he could scarcely stand it, but he rode on. Just before he arrived at his destination, the horse fell again on the other leg.

A man came along and assisted him to mount again and he rode up to his uncle's gate in Logan and called for help to get into the house. They had to cut his trousers off his swollen legs. They all said he could not start on his mission the following Friday. This was Wednesday. He had to go through the temple, so he just exercised his faith, and his uncle prayed for him and blessed him. He was a patriarch and also a regular temple ordinance worker. He told Brother Porter that Satan was trying to destroy him and keep him from fulfilling his mission.

The next morning at seven o'clock they helped him dress and they started to walk the two blocks to the temple. He fainted twice on the way, but would not give up. He went through the temple and received the blessings and the ordinances pertaining to it. When he came out of the temple his legs, although black and blue, were well and he walked without pain. He returned by horse to Salt Lake City and joined his outgoing company of missionaries. His faith had cured him.

Maggie Tolman Porter

Chapter Seven

GOD BLESSES AND HEALS

Because this is a world of travail and trouble we very often need the Lord and his blessing and healing power on our behalf. Almost daily we come in contact with our own or others' illnesses, accidents, pain, sorrow and serious problems and we have often seen and heard of miraculous healings of those who were suffering. We knew that they had been administered to and healed through the power of the holy priesthood. Most of us have received this ordinance and know that the Lord has heard the plea of the priesthood on our behalf, and through our faith we have been made whole again.

How thankful we should be to have this special blessing available to us when we live the gospel and serve the Lord. Every single day we should thank our Father in Heaven for his constant watchfulness over us, his children, and for the wonderful blessings that the priesthood brings into our lives. The following are a number of true experiences of blessings and healing.

Healed from Pneumonia

One winter day in 1908, when we were living in Porterville, Utah, I became very ill. We got the doctor, and he said that I had pneumonia in both lungs. He treated me and left medicine and instruction for my care. After he left we called in the elders to assist my husband in administering to me, as I had difficulty in breathing. I was so smothered. The men who came to assist were Bishop Durrant and Brother Thomas Phillips. They anointed my head with holy oil and blessed me, telling me I should be well from that hour. I fell asleep, and awoke perfectly well the next morning.

My husband had to go to Morgan, Utah, three miles away, which was our nearest shopping center, the next day. I accompanied him. I met the doctor on the street, and he was simply dumbfounded. He had left me the evening before with pneumonia in both lungs and a temperature of 103°. He rushed me into his office, and examined me, and found me perfectly well. He simply could not comprehend what had happened to me.

Many times in my life I have received just such blessings. In all this I humbly ask my Heavenly Father to bless me and mine according to our faith. Faith, nothing wavering, no doubting, is what gives us such results.

Maggie Tolman Porter

Her Voice Restored Through A Blessing From Harold B. Lee

My second heart operation was early in June of 1966 at a local hospital in Salt Lake City, Utah. After the first week had passed, I noticed it had become hard for me to speak. My voice was not only weak, but very high pitched. Alfred, my husband, was not a cook, and he tried to live on shredded wheat, milk and ice cream. This was bad for his sinus, so he became very deaf. He could not hear my thin, weak voice. He gave me a note-pad and pencil to write what was on my mind, so our communication was very limited. I realized that I had to eat in order to gain strength, or else I would have passed foods by, because I had no appetite—nothing tasted good. There was an awful taste in my throat. It felt like it was full of phlegm all the time and I could not get rid of it. Dr. Orme had warned me several times to be careful every time I had food in my mouth and chew it slowly, or I could easily choke to death. He said there was nothing to prevent the food particles from going right to my lungs.

In August, I had an appointment to see a throat specialist. After looking in my throat, Dr. Zobell said, "I am very sorry, your throat has been damaged in surgery and you will never be able to speak or sing again. You must be thankful to be alive!" I smiled, thinking of the blessing our son had given to me, promising that I would be able to speak and sing the songs of Zion again. The doctor, who was a church member, could only shake his head.

At this time it was very difficult for me to converse on the telephone, because my voice was barely audible on the line. On Saturday, I tried to use the telephone and found even my whisper was gone and I could only grunt spasmodically in my efforts to speak. My dear friend Maude Neeley, knew it was me. She said I must call my doctor, Dr. Mortensen. When I did so, he was not in but Dr. Rumel took the call and told me to lie back very quietly on several pillows and he would send out a prescription for me. He made an appointment for me to see the doctor the very next day.

No one but the Lord knew of my trials. Alfred came home at 7:00 p.m. and fixed supper for me and tried to comfort me, bless him.

It was Sunday, one week before Christmas. The phone rang at 2:00 p.m. and I answered it to be told by a lady that sometime earlier she had promised Alfred that she would let him know when the 17th Ward would be dedicated. The dedicatory service was that very Sunday at four o'clock! As we drove to the ward, memories flooded my mind. This was the very ward where I grew up. My youth was full of activities and my dear mother had taught me to serve the Lord and never say "No" to my dear Bishop, Nicholas G. Smith. Also, this was the ward where I met Alfred and we were married in the temple.

As we went in the chapel door, we could see the crowded condition, but there was room for the two of us, on the beautiful gold-upholstered lounge in the foyer. We looked over the lovely program to discover that Elder Harold B. Lee was to dedicate the building. He had been the president of Pioneer Stake and we knew him well. The chapel door was open wide. From where I was sitting, I could see the speakers through the inch-wide space between the door and the wall. Brother P. Melvin Peterson sang, "I Know That My Redeemer Lives". It was very special to us as he lived in the 17th Ward for many years and we knew him also.

Elder Harold B. Lee, now President Lee, was speaking. He said he wished we could see the host of people who were there from the spirit world, all of the righteous souls who had ever lived there and gone on. (Alfred whispered, "Your mother?" and I whispered, "Yes.") President Lee continued, "They have all been watching the progress of this lovely building and have been waiting for this time to come, the dedication of this building." He told of the extreme sacrifies that the elderly members had made to build this chapel. The Lord had shown his love and tender mercy to help the membership raise the money that was needed. Then Elder Lee offered a most wonderful Dedicatorial Prayer.

After the meeting was over, I whispered to Alfred that I wanted to see Elder Lee. "No," he said, "We must not bother him with all these people waiting to see him." But my "Please" must have been very convincing, because he said, "All right, but we are not going to get in this line of people who are waiting for him." I said, "That won't be necessary."

We walked down to the front of the chapel. We were standing at the base of the pulpit only seconds when Elder Lee turned around to speak to us. "Alfred, how are you?" then turning to me he said, "Alene, how are you?" Because I whispered my reply, he then turned to Alfred and asked, "Why is Alene whispering?" Alfred explained, "During the heart operation, last June, they laid the pulmonary artery out of the way and for too long at a time it had rested on the nerve that controlled the voice box. The Doctor saved her life, but in doing so, she lost her voice."

President Lee said to me, "I am so sorry." I whispered, "That is all right, Elder Lee. I have been very successful in my genealogy. The Lord has greatly blessed me." President Lee said, "And you don't need your voice for that."

Then Elder Lee took hold of my hand and in a very powerful voice said, "From this time forth, you shall receive a special blessing." I felt the warmth of his hand travel up my arm beginning at my fingertips. It was a most wonderful feeling and I did not want it to leave my body so I put my right hand in my pocket and wouldn't use it to shake hands with anyone as we went out. Our dear friends and acquaintances accepted my left hand without asking any questions.

We drove home through the bitter cold weather, but I felt warm in spite of the freezing temperature.

The next morning, I awakened early, as I had an appointment with the doctor. Our canary must have a clean cage and in so doing, I opened my mouth to whisper and my voice startled me as it came out strong and clear. I called to Alfred, "Can you hear me, honey? I am talking." He was beside me in just seconds and we cried on each other's shoulders. We realized this was the result of the special blessing that President Lee had given to me, and oh, how happy we were.

Alfred said I should call Elder Lee and let him hear me talk. I dialed his number and when he was on the line, I said, "Elder Lee, this is Alene."

"Alene, you are talking! This is a miracle, Alene, just as the Savior performed miracles when he was on the earth. The deaf were made to hear; the blind were made to see; the lame were made to walk; and the dumb were made to speak!" Then he told of the woman, who had faith if she were to touch the hem of his garment that she would be healed!

We drove to my doctor's office and I said to him, "Dr. Orme, you notice I am talking!" He said, "Say, how about that?" He prepared a pad of gauze and told me to hold it and grasp my tongue while he looked down my throat with three little mirrors. Then he was surprised! "This is remarkable! Very remarkable! The paralysis is gone! Now you won't have any worries about choking to death...the flap is *there!*" Then I told him of the wonderful event that had taken place the night before. He was so happy; he was Elder Lee's doctor, too.

Christmas came the following Sunday. According to the program outlined by the General Board, the congregation joined in singing all of the Christmas carols. Alfred started singing, but the first two notes were all he could sing, because he was listening to my voice!

I am so grateful to the Lord for that telephone call telling us of the dedication of the 17th Ward. I do not know who the lady was, but I am so grateful that we could go. I am so grateful for Alfred, for listening to me when I said, "I must see Elder Lee," so grateful that he turned around, sensing that we were there, and I am ever so grateful for this blessing that he gave to me. I can surely see that the Holy Ghost was directing all of these people so that I might receive this blessing.

Alene M. Burrell

A Newborn Child Is Healed

The second child of Brother and Sister L. Wayne Redd was born seven weeks early, on September 11, 1951. Sister Redd had tried to be very careful to do nothing to bring this little one before term. They were told that tiny Jayne would never be able to walk, nor play as other children, but would spend her life in a wheelchair, if she survived, because she had a very bad heart. Sister Redd prayed continually for this lovely infant, that she might live and be well. As the time came for the mother to leave the hospital to return home to Bountiful, Utah, baby Jayne stayed, battling for life in a humi-crib. Sadly they took leave of their baby and went home to kneel in anxious prayer. They pleaded with the Lord to make her well, to heal the ailing heart and to aid her in her struggle to survive.

When they arose, Brother Redd Said, "She's going to live and be all right." Her heart pounding with hope, Sister Redd asked, "Are you just saying that because we want it so much?" To which he answered, "No, I'm not. The spirit has testified this to me, that our baby will be all right." They were overjoyed and thanked the Lord with tears in their eyes.

The following day, when she called the hospital to see how her baby girl was, the doctor said, "We've had her out of the humidicrib for one whole minute and she didn't turn black." Sister Redd spoke up, "I can't wait until I call tomorrow and you'll probably tell me that she's well and I can bring her home."

"Oh no, she may possibly live now, but she'll never be well; she will no doubt be an invalid all her life."

The next day Sister Redd called the doctor once again and was told, "We don't know what has happened, but when we checked your baby today she was much better. Everything seems to be just fine and you can come and take her home. We just can't understand what has happened."

She thanked the doctor and the following morning went to the hospital to get Jayne and take her home. Jayne is now a mother of two and has had no trouble with a bad heart!

An Arm Healed Through Faith

Early one wet, rainy morning in 1949, young Dick Haight was hurrying along 23rd East in Salt Lake City, on his way to high school. He tried to stay off the road as much as possible and sloshed along the muddy path beside it because there were no sidewalks. He kept up a steady jogging pace as the cars passed by. Suddenly he found himself buffeted and caught up by the sleeve, hooked to the door handle of a car as it dragged him helplessly down the road.

He was taken to the hospital with an injured arm which was almost completely pulled from its socket. The doctors believed that he would never be able to use it again and were discussing how it should be placed; across his chest or hanging by his side.

Two tearful parents sought the Lord's help and prayed mightily for their son, that he might not be so badly crippled for life. They decided to call a dear friend to come and administer to him. As Brother Spencer W. Kimball gave the young man a blessing, he told him if he had enough faith, "Your arm will get better and you will be able to use it just as well as the other one." It was a marvelous blessing and promise, to which his parents responded with gratitude and hope.

The doctors wired the bones in the shoulder and put a cast on the arm. Weeks later, when they finally removed the cast, Dick was able to move his fingers. As time went on he regained more and more use of the hand and arm. While on a mission for the church, one day he felt a sharp pain in his shoulder where the bones had been wired. A local physician found a wire protruding from his arm. After having X-rays taken which showed the bones healed, he removed the wire. Today there is no apparent incapacity, but he and his family have not forgotten the Lord's special blessing to them.

A Boy Healed When Death Was Imminent

There were many marvelous healings in our family and I'd like to tell you of one of them. The winter of 1918, I was teaching school in Manderson, Wyoming. I stayed there and drove the car back for week-ends to spend time with my family. The children attended school in Otto, three miles away. They rode horses, walked, or got over that distance as best they could.

Two of my sons, Alma and Elwood, frosted their heels. Although the doctor was able to cure Elwood, Alma's heel became worse. I stopped teaching and took Alma, who was twelve at the time, down to Basin where the doctor gave it more attention. He continually became worse. The infection went up his leg. The doctor was trying his best to save the leg, but at last the flesh sluffed off the foot and an amputation was the last resort. The doctor amputated just below the knee, but the infection was already above the knee and his whole body was swelling. His temperature was 107° for more than a week.

The doctors gave him up to die—they thought he would not last until morning. We had him administered to and anointed with holy oil, time and again; but apparently to no avail. He was swollen over his entire body and the doctor said if the swelling continued, to cut the bandages and just let them go.

About ten o'clock that night he was in a pitiful condition and was simply raving. His father and Nels Winters again anointed him with oil and administered to him. Alma then fell into a gentle sleep. We watched by his bedside, expecting him to pass on easily and quietly.

Daylight came and he awakened normal. The hardness and swelling was all gone; his temperature was normal. He asked for food and ate a fair breakfast.

The doctor was sure that he was dead so did not make his regular morning call. In the afternoon, however, he had heard nothing of his death so he called. He found the boy rational, with no fever and apparently better. He told us sometimes they did that way just before death and for us not to build up hopes. But we knew that the Lord had heard our humble petitions and that our boy was going to live.

The next morning the doctor came and found Alma had slept all night. He decided that he really was better, so he changed the dressing on the leg. Although the stitches over the end of the knee had broken and the doctor suggested it be stitched again I told him that if the Lord had healed the boy, he would also heal the flesh over the amputation if the doctor would only bind the skin back over it.

The next day when the doctor dressed it again the flesh stayed up over the bone and was healing; it evidently healed a perfect wound. The doctor was a religious man; however, not a member of our church. He acknowledged that God had healed the boy, that he and our other doctor, with all their medical knowledge and skill had not expected the boy to live.

Maggie Tolman Porter

She Felt No Pain After the Operations

It sometimes seems that the Lord can send so many blessings to us that it is almost impossible to comprehend the scope of them. The special blessing of Sister Ilene Bagley was such an outstanding experience that she has thanked the Lord continually for this and all other blessings. Her husband had passed away and she was moving beyond the middle years of life when she began to have several physical problems.

One afternoon in the doctor's office it was suggested to her that she should have X-rays of her gall bladder, to which she replied, "I don't have any symptoms or problems there." "You will!" answered the doctor.

She capitulated and went in for X-rays. They showed a distended and greatly enlarged gall bladder. The physician suggested that she let him schedule surgery in the very near future. She hesitated and put off scheduling the operation. In the meantime her doctor became ill and urged her once more to go to one of his associates for the surgery. When she was examined by another doctor, he also found a lump in her breast which he said must be checked and if malignant, her breast would have to be removed. If the tumor was not malignant, they then could proceed with the gall bladder operation.

The day of the operation arrived and just before going in, her son-in-law, Robert Stone, gave her a blessing by the power of the priesthood. He told her that she would do well and come through the operation just fine. Further, he blessed her that she would feel no pain.

Although the doctor found it necessary to remove the breast, she came through the operation safely. The hemorrhaging which occurred was complicated by the heart problem so that the procedure had to be altered, but it was held under control also. The amazing thing that followed: she felt no pain and needed no medication to help her during the post-operative and recuperative period. Even the nurses were amazed.

Eleven months later, the gall bladder operation was performed, a very serious one, but it too had followed a priesthood blessing by her son-in-law, who gave her the same promises and assurances as before. This time, too, she needed no pain killers during the post-operative period, because she felt no pain. She knew that the Lord was by her side and she was thankful and grateful for his exceptional help.

A Prompting Told Her the Grandson Would Recover

In 1934, when my little grandson, Larry, came down with pneumonia, he was so ill that my daughter, Valeria, sent for me. The doctor had little hopes for his recovery. We had prayed humbly to the Lord on his behalf and I had an assurance that he would recover. His temperature was more than

105°. The doctor said that it was too high for pneumonia and that the child could not stand it much longer. When he called again that night, I told him that I knew the baby was better, but he said that all evidence was to the contrary.

Things looked mighty blue to everyone but myself. That night after the doctor left Ray, Larry's daddy, called in a neighbor and they anointed and administered to the child and he fell asleep. I persuaded Valeria and Ray to go to bed, promising that I would watch over him and if there was the least change or if he awakened, I would call them. They were very much worn out for they had no sleep for several days and nights.

Larry slept peacefully and began to breathe naturally about 3:00 a.m. He slept until sunrise, then awakened and was conscious. I called his parents and he went to his mother and was able to take food. During the night an abcess had broken in his ear. That was what had caused the terrific fever. The doctor did not know this.

Larry was healed, and soon was perfectly well again. I had received a prompting from the spirit earlier and knew for a certainty that he would get well. He had been administered to earlier by the elders before the administration performed by his father and a neighbor.

Maggie Tolman Porter

A Blessing Heals a Fractured Skull

As she gazed at her 2-1/2 year old son, Alwyn, lying on the table, bleeding from an ear, his skin a dull blue-grey, his breath coming in a rattling gurgle, Sister Edna Call begged the Lord to spare her son's life. They had had a long and difficult struggle to find and control this child's early allergies. Many times they had been frightened by these same problems, but finally, most of the struggle was over and his allergies were under control and he was a well child at last. And now, this fall of 1960, so shortly after those frightening years, to have this happen!

Just a few hours ago, they had all been enjoying a picnic and outing at Pineview Reservoir, that was before this beloved little son had fallen into the spillway. Fifteen feet his tiny form fell, to land on the concrete between the scattered broken glass. They had hastened to gather his unconscious form into their arms and return to the car and set out for a rapid trip to the hospital in Ogden, Utah.

The brain specialist was still in surgery and they were waiting for answers and help. Sister Call turned to her husband and asked him to please find someone and administer to their choice little one. Brother Call soon found an elder and returned with him. They anointed and gave Alwyn a blessing, and almost immediately the color began to return to his face. His eyes focused once more and he looked up at his parents.

X-rays confirmed that he had a badly-fractured skull. The prognosis was that he possibly would lose both his hearing and his speech. However, he rapidly improved during his ten-day stay at the hospital. He was released to return to his home in Bountiful, Utah, but on the way he began to chatter about a horse and cow that he saw. His parents were so pleased, at least he could speak! That evening his mother whispered to him, "Would you like some candy?" and he said, "Yes, I would." Both parents were grateful to a Father in Heaven who helped their son return to complete health so rapidly and were thankful for the power of the priesthood to heal the sick, for they had seen it work in their son's behalf.

The Girl Who Skirted Death

During the summer of 1917 our teen-age daughter, Valeria, had been complaining of pains in her stomach. She seemed to be growing progressively worse, so we bundled her up and drove her to the hospital in Basin, Wyoming where the doctors said that she had tuberculosis of the bowels. As she became more ill and listless, we despaired for her life and called in the Elders to administer to her. Her father, Brother May and her Uncle Myron gave her a blessing. They rebuked the destroyer and bade her be made well again.

All three of the doctors believed that she was dying and held little hope for her recovery. When she responded to the administration and rapidly overcame the dreaded peritonitis which was threatening her life, the doctors were filled with amazement and from that time on, they called her "the girl that was dead, but came back to life." Our family rejoiced at this God-given help through His priesthood and praised the Lord for His goodness.

Later in life, she was once again spared when her first child was born and her life hung in the balance, a true second miracle on her behalf.

Maggie Tolman Porter

Blessed to be a Mother

Prayerfully, Sister Ilene Bagley, who was childless after several years of marriage, went to the Lord for help. She had been to several doctors, had a number of tests, and followed the advice given to her. It was all to no avail. She was very sad, for her heart longed greatly to have a child.

One day she was talking to her husband and said, "I believe I'll go to Bishop Smith and ask for a blessing. So many people say that he has the gift of healing." He had been her bishop before she went on her mission and at this particular time was a counselor in the Salt Lake Temple presidency.

She made an appointment and went in to see him and requested a blessing so that she might be able to have a baby because they were so anxious to have a family. President Nicholas G. Smith smiled at her in his sweet, loving way and said, "Sister Bagley, have you done all you can?"

"If you mean have I been to several doctors, followed instructions, tried to find out the trouble and found none, prayed about it and wept a lot, yes, I have done all I can!"

He answered her, "Then I am certain that it is in the Lord's hands. I'll give you a blessing." The beautiful blessing he gave to her promised that she would have a child and become a mother in Zion. She was overjoyed and thankful to the Lord, for she knew the blessing would be fulfilled.

Within a short time, she found herself expecting a baby and was almost overcome with happiness and joy. A lovely baby girl came into their hearts and home and they thanked the Lord for His goodness.

A few years later, unable to conceive again, she went to President Smith for a second blessing, following which the Lord once again blessed her and she bore a second lovely daughter.

Sometime after the birth of her second child, President Smith, who was by then an assistant to the twelve apostles, was taken in death and mourned by all who knew him.

As the years passed on this sister prayed mightily to the Lord that she might be blessed with another baby. The Lord heard and answered and for the third time she knew the joy of expecting a little one. Another beautiful daughter was born to them and life was good, and they raised their children with thankful hearts.

A Husband Assured by the Blessing He Gave His Wife

As they were getting ready to leave for the hospital in Salt Lake City, Utah, prior to the birth of each of their children, Brother J. Courtney Black would give his wife a special blessing, to protect her and to assure the safe delivery of their child. As the due date for their fourth child arrived, December 16, 1971, Brother Black was giving his wife a blessing when through inspiration, he told her that she would be faced with a serious problem during the birth of this baby, but she need not fear for herself, nor the child, because they would come safely through the experience. They were surprised, but the spirit testified to them and they felt comforted, knowing that the Lord's help and guidance would be with them and with the doctor in the forthcoming event.

During the birth period, Brother Black was beside his wife in the labor room. He was a bit apprehensive, but not anxious, as he followed the advanced labor and birth of their child. Suddenly he noticed a look of concern and fear on the doctor's face; Mr. Black was asked to leave the labor room and to wait outside by the nurse's station. The moment had come! He had no idea what the problem was, but he had full trust in the Lord and absolutely knew that she and the baby would come through all right! With this calm assurance, he waited, and the wondering nurses noted that he seemed almost unconcerned. He knew he had no cause for alarm—he was prepared, he had complete faith in the Lord. And he was right! Later, he learned that the dread placenta previa had occurred, where the premature loosening of the placenta ofttimes caused fatal hemorrhaging. The doctor had been able to cope with the problem and get it under control so that the baby boy was safely born and the mother's life protected.

Healed from a Horse's Kick

As a young man in 1908, Irvin McDonald was doing his chores one day when he was kicked in the abdomen by a horse. As he was struggling in great pain, a neighbor was sent for to come and administer to him. Brother William G. Wagstaff lived a few blocks away from their home in Salt Lake City, Utah, but he hurried to the boy's home. He administered to Irvin and gave him a blessing that he might recover from the severe blow and possible internal injuries that he had received. Almost immediately, the pain left him and he was healed. Their mother watched closely for further complications from the accident, but the healing had been complete, and there were no further problems.

Irvin had been miraculously healed by the administration and the family thanked the Lord for His loving help.

Cancer Cured by a Missionary's Blessing

Sister Dolores Clarkson recalls that as she was growing up her mother told her the following story about her grandmother, Suzanne Christensen.

As a young mother living in Denmark in 1875, Suzanne had contracted a growth on the left side of her face which finally was diagnosed as cancer. It continued to increase in size. They were much alarmed, especially since she was expecting a child. One day, her young daughter came to her and told her about some neighbors who had been visited by L.D.S. missionaries. "Mother, why don't you ask the missionaries to heal you? I've heard Mrs. J. tell of many people who have been healed when the missionaries blessed them."

The young expectant mother talked with her husband, the neighbors, and then asked the missionaries if they would administer to her. They anointed and blessed her, promising that she would be made well. Within a short time the growth began to shrink and after a while was gone completely. Thanking her Father in Heaven for this great blessing they began to investigate the church. Soon she, her husband, her family and her sister joined the church.

They then made plans to come to Utah and soon were on their way to the Salt Lake valley where they raised their family strong in the church. Her sister, who had joined the church came with them. She spent a great deal of her life working on genealogy and doing temple work for the dead.

Set Apart to Bless the Sick with Her Prayers

In September, 1902, while we were visiting my sister, Mattie, her husband, Emery, and their family in Logan, Utah, my daughter, Rhea, came down with pneumonia. She was 18 months old at the time. We had a very good doctor, who also happened to be L.D.S., but Rhea became worse with meningitis. The doctor said that she could not possibly live, that she was really dying then.

We had the elders several times, but she seemed no better. Because of the loss of her little sister, Viola, I did not have much faith at that time. I believed she would die too. My husband felt the same way, so we were sitting around the crib, waiting for the end. Her eyes were set, her head drawn back, her whole spine as rigid as it could be.

A knock came at the door. Mattie answered it and soon walked in with a dear old white-haired sister by the name of Needum. I remember how it vexed me for a stranger to intrude on us at that hour of sorrow. In a moment she told us that she had been impressed to come and bless our sick child. She asked if she might pray. Of course we told her she could, but added that the child was dying, and that it was too late. She told us she had been set apart in the temple to bless the sick with her prayers, and if the Lord saw fit, it was never too late.

We knelt around the little bed. I will never forget that marvelous prayer and what it accomplished. I had hold of one of Rhea's little hands and her daddy the other one. Her eyes were glazed in death. The good sister first asked the Lord to give the parents of this little child faith. She said that for some reason, she knew not why, we had no faith. She prayed on, and before she finished the prayer, Rhea opened her eyes naturally and gripped our hands and smiled. In less than an hour we had her dressed and she was playing with her daddy's watch. She ate some milk toast and an egg. She had taken nothing for more than a week. She was healed. Of course she was too weak to walk, but she tried.

That night the doctor called and said that he had not been informed of her death. When he came in, Rhea was laughing and playing with her toys. I never saw a man so surprised! When he examined her that morning he said she was dying, so that a miracle was surely performed in her behalf because she was well and happy, now.

Maggie Tolman Porter

Two Daughters Healed

Not one, but two miraculous healing experiences occurred in the Beth Gore family of Bountiful, Utah. Gail had been ill a great deal that winter of 1965 and just couldn't seem to get well even though they had the elders administer to her. They were at their wits end. At last Sister Gore said, "I think we need a second administration for Gail and *then* she will get well." With great faith, she once more called in the elders and had her daughter blessed. During the administration, one of the brothers said, "We bless you that you will be made whole and you will be made well if you will cease to take all medication." Faithfully, following those inspired instructions, Gail made enormous strides to sound health and soon was free from her illness.

In January, 1971, a second daughter, Rebecca, awakened with a bad pain in her stomach. She was taken to the doctor who, following a blood count, diagnosed it as appendicitis. His recommendation was to remove it as soon as possible. Sister Gore was impressed to take her daughter home and have an administration performed. The doctor counseled her, "You must not wait very long, it is too dangerous."

Rebecca was taken home and a neighbor was called in to administer to her. He told her that she would get well and that her doctor would know what to do. Following a phone call to the doctor, Rebecca was taken to the hospital. After checking her again, the doctor decided not to operate until morning, however they would keep a very close watch on her.

The following morning the doctor called her at six o'clock and said that Rebecca was completely out of danger. He and Sister Gore were certain that the administration was responsible for this miracle. She knew that without the Lord's help Rebecca would certainly have had an operation, so she gratefully thanked the Lord for his assistance.

Lifted from the Floor as He Sealed the Anointing

In the fall of 1959 an eight-year-old girl lay in the intensive care unit of a Salt Lake City hospital. She was near death as the result of a serious automobile accident. Her mother, who had been driving the car, was killed in the same accident, but her younger sister, luckily, was uninjured. A grieving father now hovered over his little daughter with fear in his heart and tears in his eyes. Although he was not a Latter-day Saint, he had seen and heard of the power of the priesthood and now asked for someone to administer to his little girl. Two elders were called in to perform the administration. As they placed their hands on her head, they noted that her skin was cold and damp as she lay there unconscious. They were fearful that she was too far gone to be helped, but began by anointing her. When Brother Henry Bredthauer started to seal the anointing, he suddenly felt lifted from the floor and felt as if he was hung in midair all through the blessing. Through the power of the priesthood they blessed her to become well and take up her life once again. They both had felt the strong power flowing as this blessing was pronounced. When they looked down at the little girl, they felt that now, she did have a chance to live.

They were told by the father, later, that the girl had regained consciousness the next morning and had made rapid strides toward getting well and he was overjoyed.

A short time later the father married again, and also joined the church where he is actively engaged in church work.

Prompted How to Stop the Hemorrhage

When I was a young mother, in the fall of 1901, I was asked by a little woman that did not belong to the church if I would be there at her place to help the midwife when her baby came in about six weeks. We were her nearest neighbors and her husband was gone a great deal because he ran a freighting outfit to Thermopolis, Wyoming and to Red Lodge Mountain. She was alone with her little six-year-old boy. She sent the little fellow out in the middle of the night for me, and asked that I get someone to drive up to Burlington for a midwife, which I did. Uncle Milton went. He had to go a mile and a half, catch a team and drive twelve miles and back.

When I returned to her home with her little boy, she was almost dead from hemorrhage. Her mattress was filled with straw. She had bled so much that it had run through the bed and down on the floor, leaving a strip of blood six or eight inches wide below the foot of the bed. She was so weak she could hardly speak.

I knelt down beside her and asked God to tell me what to do. The answer came to me as plainly as if someone had spoken. "Take vinegar and alcohol and place a cold compress across her lower body."

I asked her if she had alcohol and vinegar. She nodded toward the cupboard. I grabbed a towel and made the compress. It stopped the hemorrhage instantly.

The midwife arrived after several hours and the baby was born dead. This, however, saved the mother's life. She was very delicate, anaemic, and the terrible loss of blood proved too much. She also had a bad heart which in the end took her life in a short time.

Maggie Tolman Porter

A Blessing Overcame Her Depression

Sister Grace Fillerup was going through a period of depression. Long years of hard work had taken their toll; she was the busy mother of ten children and was not at top peak physically in the spring of 1936. Because the depression seemed to continue, she went to her bishop, Owen L. Alphen of Lovell West Ward in Wyoming. After she told him how she had been feeling, she asked for a special blessing. He placed his hands on her head and gave her a blessing with promises of relief. He told her, "Be of good cheer, Sister Fillerup. Your boys will grow up and go to school and on missions. All will be well with you." As this blessing was pronounced on her she literally felt a load lifted from her heart and her mind. In the days ahead, not only was she free from the oppressive feelings through which she had been going, but things seemed to move along much more smoothly and with fewer problems occurring in the family. This was a testimony to her and strengthened her resolve to keep all the laws and commandments as the Lord wanted her to.

Administration Brings Cancer Cure

In 1958 Sister Della Gabbitas of Bountiful, Utah, had an experience with a very serious illness which she knows would have taken her life without the intervention of her Father in Heaven. She had been working taking care of children for a family, when she began to feel ill. At first there were no specific symptoms except that she just did not feel well. After a time, when more severe symptoms arose, she went to the doctor who thought she might have cancer of the cervix. Before the diagnosis was complete, she found herself so tired that she was forced to give up her job. At that point she became ill enough to be hospitalized for a biopsy, which was then followed by an operation. The doctor found that she had a tumor in her left side which was cancerous. Since it was found to be inoperable because blood vessels were in the way, the incision was closed and the decision was made not to tell her of the cancer. At that time the doctor's prognosis was that she might possibly live from a year to a maximum of five years.

As time went on and she became progressively more miserable, she had an inkling that she must have cancer. Both her mother and brother had died with it, and she feared that this was the basis for her illness also. Until then she had not let herself think of such a possibility.

She called in a beloved friend of the family who was both a doctor and a bishop and asked him to administer to her, which he gladly agreed to do. His prayer began, "Our Father in Heaven has told us unless we are appointed unto death, we can be healed. Realizing this, we command you to be healed from the crown of your head to the soles of your feet, something that even the physicians and scientists have not been able to do for you. But remember that our Father in Heaven is the great physician, so do not worry about your health. You will be made well."

The following week she returned to her doctor for an examination and he could not find the lump in her side, but he cautioned her not to get too excited. At that point she asked him if she had cancer and he said "Yes," then carefully explained to her how cancer works in the body. The following week the radiologist declared, "I couldn't be more pleased at how your condition has improved." Then her doctor told her that the tests taken were all negative and added, "Two weeks ago, the lump was there, and now, a week after your administration, it is gone." She has shared this story with many friends and with others in testimony meetings and is forever grateful to the Lord.

Chapter Eight

GOD GIVES DREAMS AND VISIONS

Another way in which the Father gives us help, guidance or direction is through dreams and visions. Dreams are direction given to us while we are asleep. Sometimes they are subject to interpretation; other times the lesson experienced is plain and clear cut. Visions appear to one while he is awake and are more clear than dreams and have more of the element of reality while occurring. However, there are times when a person does not know which he has experienced. The individual may think that he was asleep when he experienced the vision, when in fact he actually was awake. He may think at the time or afterwards that the experience was un-real, but still know that it truly did happen and was sent by the Lord.

Quoting the first sentence of one of our latest scriptual additions, which was a vision given to the Prophet Joseph Smith in the Kirtland Temple, January 21, 1836, he says, "The heavens were opened upon us, and I beheld the celestial kingdom of God, and the glory thereof, whether in the body or out I cannot tell...." This statement tells us that a vision is so glorious that it is difficult in some cases, to even know if one is in the body or out of it. The following experiences stand as the individuals reported them, either a dream or a vision.

Directions in a Dream

A sacred incident that happened to me occurred early on the morning of February 20, 1964. I had been busily engaged in preparing my genealogy book for publication. I was employed at the Tooele Utah Army Depot at the time, and spent many hours working on the project from the time I got home until midnight, then up again by 2:00 a.m. and worked until 6:00 a.m., when I had to get ready to go to work. My husband and I were having quite a controversy over what we would have to charge for the books, in order to come out anywhere near even on the paper cost, etc. Of course I had no idea how to judge the cost for the book, and I figured about $3.50 would be high. He said that I would have to charge at least $5.00...so we argued about it quite a bit. I was hurrying to get the book finished before I would go into the hospital for lung surgery and it was growing by leaps and bounds. Over a hundred people had sent their money in at my original estimate of $3.50, and many more requests were coming in.

Early one morning I had a very vivid dream in which I saw myself talking to President McKay on the telephone and he was giving me specific instructions about my book. It ended up with my being able to see him in the telephone as we conversed. He was shaking his finger at me, and being very decisive in his instructions. He said, "Don't you take less than $5.00 for any one of those books." I awoke with a feeling that I had actually been talking to him and gave the higher price serious thought from then on.

Maxine Pace

His Mission Was Beyond Death

When my beloved brother, Orson, was nineteen years old (in 1891), he died of diptheria. From his childhood he had always said that when he was nineteen years old he was going on a mission. Of course, it was the joy of a mother's heart to have him feel that way.

That summer there had been diptheria in the home of a family in Salt Lake who had sent a trunk of clothing to a relative in our town in Star Valley, Wyoming. In about ten days one of the children became ill and lived only a few hours and soon there were twenty deaths in a town of less than one hundred fifty people. There was no doctor within forty miles and there was no quarantine.

We had the mail contract at that time, carrying mail from Star Valley to Montpelier, Idaho. It took three days, or parts of three days, to make the trip. Orson went with the mail as usual. He was feeling all right when he left. He took sick in the night. He hooked up his team and pulled into Montpelier in the early morning. He went straight to a doctor who took one look and would not even let him inside his office. There was no hospital there either. The doctor ordered him out of town immediately. They did, however, load the mail sacks in his buckboard and he spent another night in the canyon.

While in that canyon that night he beheld a vision of what his mission was to be. It was to be on the other side of the veil, beyond death. He was very happy about all that was shown him, and never wanted them to try to cure him. Although he wanted the elders to administer to him, he would give his consent only if they would pray the Lord to take him in peace, and quickly.

He lived ten days after taking ill. He became very hoarse, but apparently was recovering from the disease. He walked from one room to another. He said he wanted to die in mother's bed. Whenever one of us were ill, it did us so much good if we could go to mother's bed.

The good old brother whom Orson had called to bless him came and Orson told him just what to tell the Lord. We all kneeled about the bed while Brother Jensen prayed. I shall never forget that prayer: pleading that God would be merciful to such a fine young man. When we arose Brother Jensen took the oil and was about to anoint Orson. "Wait a minute," Orson whispered. Then he took mother's hand and asked her not to mourn for him, that he was just going on that mission. He bade her goodbye, smiled at all of us, and turned his face to the wall and went to sleep, to awaken on that brighter shore.

He was a boy without guile. He always served the Lord and studied the gospel from the time he could read, preparing his mind for that mission he was going on when he was nineteen!

Maggie Tolman Porter

His Former Wife Returned to Encourage Their Marriage

Brother Will Harston lost his wife, Clara, in 1915 and was struggling to manage his family of five children. During the months following his wife's death, he had some help from neighbors and friends in this small town in Wyoming, but he knew he must begin to look for a mother for his little family. He wrote to Mary Briggs, who was Clara's brother's widow who lived in Bountiful, Utah, to thank her for her sympathetic letters following Clara's death. Mary responded, but hesitantly. Several friends had said to her, "You ought to marry Will and help him raise those children," but she did not agree with them. She felt her responsibility was to raise *her* three children.

After a short time, she set aside all thoughts of marrying Will, until one night she had a strange dream. In it, her deceased sister-in-law, Clara, was standing beside her husband, Will, and as she watched, Clara beckoned her to come and stand on the other side of Will. Mary immediately knew what Clara had in mind—that she should marry Will—and she said to her, "No, I won't," and she seemed to turn as the dream faded. When she awoke she thought about the dream. She was sure that her answer was still, "No, I won't." After all, he was her brother-in-law, or more correctly her sister-in-law's husband, and that was always the way she thought of him.

Her dreams were not to be stilled on the subject, however, for another night she saw herself holding out her hand, palm up. Glancing into the hand she saw her three children's faces. She stared at them and said, "Why, there's room for more children there."

Following this dream, she was a little alarmed, for the first dream was still fresh in her mind and she found that she presently could not think about Will in a romantic sense. Whether or not Will had any such dreams as she, is not known, but he did begin to court Mary. Slowly her feelings about him changed, and eventually they were married and teamed up her three, his five, and at last their four, to make a very happy family.

They were not the only ones happy, for Mary had still another dream in which Clara returned, radiantly happy, and told Mary, "I want to thank you so much. Now I can do my work without worrying about my family." She left with a beautiful sweet smile.

A Dream Helped Her Discern Her True Love

When a girl has a boy friend on a mission—one that she really likes but is not engaged to, there are lots of questions she asks herself. This happens especially when another "extra nice" young man comes along and she is dating him. Jayne Redd had dated Marty Kearl for several months before he went on his mission. They had much in common—their interests were similar, they laughed about the same things, and had the same dislikes. Yes, they really got along great, but there had been no serious talk of marriage. Their relationship was left on a "wait and see" basis.

After a year and a half, she found herself attracted to Rick who was a returned missionary and a very special person. Of course their friendship was different than her's and Marty's—not nearly as exciting, but great all the same. Her question was what to do? Maybe she, like lots of other girls who had hopefully waited for a missionary's return and then been disappointed, could have the same thing happen to her. So was it wise to hope and keep waiting? She wasn't just keeping Rick on the string, just in case, she truly liked him and didn't know what to do.

Jayne turned to the Lord for help, and asked for assistance in her deciding what to do before she got too interested in Rick, so that she would make the right choice. The answer was not long in coming. She had a special dream that very night. Jayne saw herself being married to Rick in a beautiful temple ceremony followed that evening by a lovely reception. She was so happy! Then Marty came home from his mission and she went to hear his homecoming talk and when she saw him a great anguish came into her soul, "Oh, how could this be? I have married the wrong man!" and she awoke from this dream feeling so frustrated that she was almost weeping. Then, she knew that the Lord was guiding her, telling her what to do, showing her that Marty was the right one for her.

When her beloved Marty came home, they both knew that they wanted to spend eternity together and they were soon engaged. Not long afterward they were married in the Salt Lake Temple.

Joseph Smith Sent Him to David Whitmer

When my mother who was born in 1880 was a small child, her father, Carry Frisbey, had a choice spiritual experience. One night as he lay sleeping in their home in Braidwood, Illinois, he had a dream in which the Prophet Joseph Smith appeared to him and told him that he was wanted in Richmond, Missouri. He was directed to go to Denver, Colorado first, where he would be met by another man. They were then to proceed to Richmond to see David Whitmer. At the time, my mother had just recovered from an attack of the measles and two tiny brothers were ill with the disease. Grandfather hesitated leaving grandmother with the children ill, but she told him that he should go.

Arriving at the Denver station, he stepped out onto the depot platform and a man came up to him and asked what was wanted of him. They had never met before. The man introduced himself as John Jacob Snyder. He told Grandpa that he had been told to meet the train and a man with a full, bushy beard would meet him and tell him what to do. Since Grandpa was not financially well off at the moment, he decided to ask a friend to go with Mr. Snyder. When the arrangements were made, Grandpa stayed in Illinois while that others proceeded to Richmond, Missouri. They met with David Whitmer, who told them that he had promised the Lord that he would make a statement of his beliefs and his testimony. He called it his "living testimony" of the Book of Mormon and asked John J. Snyder to write it for him, which he did.

Grandpa and Mr. Snyder remained friends for the rest of their lives. Both participated in a religious organization called the Church of Christ or Whitmerite Church. Grandfather moved to Provo, Utah in 1888, acting as a missionary for the Whitmerite Church. The family lived in Provo and in Salt Lake City where Grandpa did sculpture and tombstone work until his death in Salt Lake on October 11, 1895. When he was on his deathbed he said, "I should have joined the Mormon Church, I'm sorry I didn't." All of the family later joined the L.D.S. Church.

Norma C. Larsen

A Manifestation Foreshadowed the Child's Death

We lost our second child, Viola, in September 1898 when she was one year and nine days old. She died of mastoid ear. Today they would operate and save her life, but in those days they did not perform that kind of operation except in the large cities, at some big hospital—and we lived in a small town in Wyoming. Before she died I had a very strange manifestation regarding her. It makes the perspiration almost come to my brow even yet, just to recall it.

I had employed a dear fifteen-year-old girl, Annie, to stay with me while my husband was away and to help me clean house. That particular morning Annie told me that she did not feel very well, and that she wanted to go home and plant the flower seeds I had given her. She lived just across the field. She went home, and lay down to rest while her daddy prepared the soil for her flowers.

Later in the day her brother came for me, saying they could not awaken Annie. I went over, but she died in a few hours.

The next night I had a terrible manifestation. My husband was away hunting cattle so I was alone. I was wide awake, nursing little Viola. This was a short time before she took sick. It was just breaking daylight when I heard a slight noise at my north bedroom window. I was almost frightened stiff. I raised up on my elbow to see what made the noise, and watched three white coffins come in at that window. The two larger ones passed on through the house, but the third one, the smaller one, seemed to stand on two chairs by that window. Something told me it was little Viola's coffin. I buried my face in the pillow and wept bitterly; then I looked up in a minute and it was gone.

I was still crying when Uncle Myron walked in with my milk. He always milked when my husband was away. I was simply in hysterics. He had to take me and the children up to his place. I just couldn't seem to get over it.

We soon heard that old Sister Campbell was dead, and we already knew that Annie had died, but that third little coffin was still unaccounted for. They all told me it was because I was so nervous that I had just imagined it. But I didn't imagine it—I saw it. Why, I do not know. But it made me nearly sick.

When little Viola did become ill I did not have one bit of faith—I knew she would die. When they carried her little coffin, they set it just as I had seen it, by the north window, on two chairs, and Viola's death was the next death in the ward.

Maggie Tolman Porter

She Chose Her Son's Death
Rather than His Life as an Invalid

Sister Lucille Clark slept heavily, but fitfully. She was bowed down with fear and grief as her eldest son, at age 19, lay gravely ill in the hospital intensive care unit, at San Francisco, California. He was suffering with acute pylo-nephritis. It was December, 1948.

In her dreams a voice spoke. She was told that she could keep her son or let him return to his heavenly home. If he lived he would never be able to work again—he would be a hopeless invalid. Then she saw her son lying in a casket. Once more the voice told her that the choice was hers. She answered, "Rather than see him unhappy as an invalid, and unable to do any work, I would rather that he be taken home. I know that he would be very miserable if he could not work, and he would be so unhappy if I had to work to support him. I know I must give him up." She awakened from this dream crying, yet she was somewhat resigned to that which she felt was inevitable.

Two days later her son passed away and she knew that the Lord would help her somehow to accept this loss, for already the dream had prepared her. She had been given a choice to make and had accepted his death as being the wiser and better choice for her son's peace of mind and happiness. It was a decision she could live with, grievous though it was, and she thanked God for helping her throughout this time of sorrow.

He Saw the Happiness of the Spirit World

A dear brother in the church, Ivan Harris, came from a very close-knit and cooperative family who took great pride and joy in the accomplishments of the family members. Happiness was found in sharing the rewards of diligence and of active church service. Among the members of this family was a young man, a nephew, who found it harder to adhere strictly to the mores of our society and had strayed some from church participation. For this deviation from the family goals he was looked upon by this dear brother as a kind of "black sheep"—certainly he did not seek the same rewards in the world or in the church.

In June 1973, this dear brother became acutely ill and lapsed into a coma from which the family was certain he would not recover. While in this coma, he experienced a vision of things as they were in the spirit world. While in vision he felt great happiness and joy and was struck by the almost overwhelming spirit of love that literally permeated the atmosphere of the place. As a joyous, happy feeling came over him he suddenly thought of his nephew toward whom he felt such angry feelings. "Oh, I cannot bear to be in such a wonderfully joyous place and feel all the love and caring that is here and continue to think such uncharitable and angry thoughts about my nephew." He begged to be allowed to set aright this estrangement between him and his nephew.

Permission was granted and upon gaining consciousness he asked for his nephew. He left a message, asking that his nephew be told that he loved him and forgave him. Following this, he lived for eight days and then passed away.

Vision Foretells Birth Complications

Back in 1939, Sister Winona Hammond was expecting her first baby and was happily making plans for the coming advent. She and her mother, who were very close to each other, were making plans to share even that special moment of the birth of her baby.

Sister Hammond lived in Salt Lake City and her mother lived in Draper, Utah. As the time moved along they decided that she should go to her Mother's home to have the baby. In those depression years many women had their babies at home and this was what she was planning to do also. The doctor agreed that he would be there for the delivery of their first tiny infant and the family was looking forward to that special day!

In January,1940, about a month before the baby was due, her mother came to her and suggested that she have the baby in the hospital instead of at her home, saying that it was better for the first child to be born with proper facilities available. Sister Hammond felt rather hurt that her mother had changed her mind about having her deliver the baby in her home, and was disappointed because for months she had looked happily forward to being with her mother when the baby came. Her mother, aware that her daughter was feeling hurt, decided to tell her the reason for the suggested change of plans. "I didn't want to tell you, for fear you'd become alarmed, but I had a dream last night and in it was a warning. The dream was so vivid that I knew you should not try to have the baby at home, but that you should go to the hospital instead."

"Oh, Mother, if you have had one of your warnings, I know that it is surely the right thing to do and we will make plans to go to the hospital."

When her baby came on the 7th of February she hemorrhaged badly and had to find blood donors. Her mother could not give blood to her because she had pernicious anemia, but her father gave blood, not once, but twice, to save her life. She went into shock, but finally rallied and the bleeding was at last controlled. The baby had much difficulty breathing, despite the artificial respiration, and they had to place her in a resuscitator before her breathing came naturally.

Later her mother told her that she dreamed that she had died, but dared not tell her. They were both thankful that they had heeded the warning dream which saved her life and they appreciated the Lord's goodness to them.

Chapter Nine

GOD ALLOWS VISITATIONS
FROM BEYOND THE VEIL

After experiencing a visitation from a spirit, some people actually doubt their own sanity. Sometimes it is hard for them to believe that they have been blessed with such a special manifestation, or they argue that such things just do not happen. Some think they are unworthy of the Lord's help, at least to *that* extent, and they find it difficult to accept such a blessing. Ofttimes a *visual* visit is more convincing. Even then, after it is over, some may not be able to accept it for awhile, but think they must have imagined it. One thing I am certain of is that visitations are part of the Lord's ongoing love and concern for us and they are not as uncommon as one might think.

There are certain guidelines about receiving visitations or so the leaders of the church have told us since the beginning of the church. One of them is that we should not seek for a sign. Our faith must precede the miracle. We cannot think to gain faith by asking the Lord for a miracle. Instead, we must have faith that the Lord, in his wisdom, will provide many miracles for us as he deems them desirable or necessary to our growth toward perfection. We should not insist that our wisdom is greater than God's. Until we have this perfect faith in him, we will, by this very lack of faith, deprive ourselves of many special blessings. If we desire "exceptional" help from the Lord, we have every right to pray for it. If our desire is righteous, we, in the Lord's own due time, will receive the blessing, if he deems it in our best interest.

He Returned to Ask that His Temple Work be Done

In June, 1906, young John McDonald a native of Salt Lake City, Utah, passed away at the age of 19 years. During his teen years he had been such an active, athletic, and enthusiastic young man that he had excelled in many sports. So zealous was he, that he had developed what was called athletes heart, which slowed him somewhat in his physical activities. During the summer, he worked driving a water wagon, but unfortunately he developed tuberculosis, to which ailment, complicated by the heart damage, he succumbed.

A few months after his death he appeared to his sister Flora saying, "Look at my clothes. I can't do the work I want to do because I haven't had my temple work done." She told her parents about the visitation and they talked of getting the endowments done for him, but in the press of daily work, they let the matter rest, if only temporarily.

Within a few months, John once again visited his sister Flora, to ask her if they couldn't get his temple work done, so he could do his work. After this urgent plea, they worked and planned and were overjoyed to get John's endowments completed in September 1907, just fifteen months after his death.

Shortly after his temple work was done, John reappeared to his sister. This time happiness and joy radiated from his being and he said, "Thank you very much. Now, I can do what I am supposed to do."

Her Husband Comforted Her on Their Anniversary

The doorbell rang. Mrs. Venice Mendelsohn went to the door this spring day of 1975, to find a policeman on the doorstep. Feeling surprised and flustered, she invited him in and asked him to be seated. He settled his large frame onto the couch and turned almost apologetically to her. "I'm afraid that I have some bad news for you Mrs. Mendelsohn." Her eyes focused on his face as fear and anxiety alternated in her breast. "Your husband was shot in a holdup at the service station where he works. He was alone at the time and we don't have details of the holdup, because he is unconscious. They've taken him to the hospital. I'll be glad to drive you there if you'd like."

"Oh, dear heavens, I hope it isn't too serious!" she almost wept as she gazed pleadingly at the officer, hoping for some assurance that her beloved husband was not going to die. He told her that he did not know, but the doctor could tell her more.

On the way to the hospital she questioned him about the shooting, "Do you know where my husband was wounded?"

"I'm sorry, but I never did see him, so I can't say. A customer came in and phoned the police when he discovered your husband lying on the floor of the station."

That afternoon about 4:30 she left the hospital, stricken with grief, for Chuck had succumbed to the bullet wounds he had suffered. Tears poured down her face and she wiped them away with several tissues. Her brother held her arm and she turned to cry on his shoulder. When they were in the car she moaned, "Oh, I don't think I can stand it. He was so good and we were so happy." He tried to comfort her as he drove.

Many memories of this time clung to her as the days and weeks passed, until she became almost bitter. Hadn't she had enough trials and problems? Almost eleven years ago, she had lost her husband in a drowning accident and suffered through that time before meeting her beloved Chuck. It was true they had had a very happy marriage and things had been going fine for them; the children were almost grown. As she thought of living without him her unhappiness grew and she became almost ill. Actually she did become ill; her arthritis which had been troublesome before was so greatly aggravated that she was sometimes bedridden with it. Her health, which had not been robust for many years, seemed to multiply with problems as she grieved, and as she struggled less and less her life became more difficult.

One night, as she lay in her bed, her thoughts turned once again to her husband, this time with an even greater intensity and sadness because it was their special day—their tenth wedding anniversary! Suddenly Chuck was with her. No, she thought, it could not be! It must be her imagination. But then she heard him speak; "Dearest, you must not grieve so. You must try to be well, you must rise up from your bed and take up the threads of your life and care for the children and find a new life. I left this earth because it is a necessary part of our growth, and even if I could return I would not do so, because this was meant to be. Take strength in your sister, Norma. You have the same strength, but you don't use it."

She couldn't believe her ears. Oh, she must be hallucinating! But surely that was his voice speaking to her. Her grief sprang anew and she wept once more. Soon, she ceased crying and a wondering came over her. Could this actually be Chuck talking to her, telling her to begin life anew? Or was she losing her mind? It had been so clear, she protested.

She rose to her feet and called her sister to tell her and to receive, if possible, some reassurance of her sanity. When she reminded her sister that it was her wedding anniversary, she said how terribly she missed him and how full of grief she was at his loss. Before she could tell her of Chuck's visit, her sister told her, "After my husband died, he came and talked to me and comforted me."

"Then I'm not losing my mind!" Mrs. Mendelsohn cried, to which her sister said, "Did your husband talk to you too?" and she then told her sister about the experience and felt so greatly relieved to be able to believe that Chuck had actually talked to her, and it was true.

They discussed the reasons for the visit and the rapport between these sisters grew as they thankfully acknowledged that this experience was a great comfort at a time of sorrow. Mrs. Mendelsohn resolved to, at least, try and accept her loss and move into a new life.

Visit From a Fisherman Father

Every time I look back on the beautiful experience I had in the summer of 1973 I have to cry. It's not that it was a sad thing, but rather it was so touchingly beautiful. My husband and I and the children were camping out one weekend down at Fish Lake in Utah. The fish were biting and after my husband cleaned his catch, I was standing at the picnic table cooking them on a griddle over the Coleman stove. Suddenly I was aware that someone was standing behind me watching me and I was rather amused to think that my husband would just stand there without a word, watching as I prepared the fish for dinner. My amusement turned to amazement as I spotted my husband coming down the trail opposite. Instantly my head swiveled and for a brief instant saw my father standing there before he faded out of sight. I was quite shook up, but also mighty pleased; Daddy had died when I was seven years of age. I remembered he had been a great fisherman also, and he loved to camp out. Now it seemed to me that he had returned to see his little girl, grown up, enjoying the same kind of activity.

We sat down and I told my husband of the experience— what a special boon—and he said to me, "Your Dad would have enjoyed an outing like this, and the fact that he did come and watch you seems to be saying it meant something special to him." It is so humbling to have an experience like this, but such a 'specially happy one too, that I shall never forget it.

Norma Burton

A Husband Comforts His Wife

It was a second marriage for each of them; she was a convert to the church, had been divorced, and for years worked to support a sweet little daughter. He also had a little daughter, had been a widower, and this marriage, which had been solemnized in the temple, was a very happy and rewarding one for both of them. Busy and active in church work in Bountiful, Utah, they both thrived and felt that life was good. She was overjoyed to have someone who truly loved and cared for her—it seemed as though her whole life had been waiting for this time. Her mother died when she was but ten years of age, and she had married young and, unfortunately, this marriage turned out very badly and she was soon left alone to work and raise her child alone.

After twelve happy years of her truly wonderful marriage to Brother Les Bryant, he became ill and rapidly sank until he passed away in a short time. What a blow to lose her beloved companion, more especially because they had both felt so secure in thinking that they had a long life together ahead of them because his patriarchal blessing had promised that he would have a long and happy life. It is true those twelve years had been exceptionally happy. But long? Oh, no, and he was barely in his early fifties when he died. It just wasn't easy to accept.

The days and weeks passed and one day a scant two months after his death she sat thinking: things did not seem to be getting much easier. In fact, she felt more resentment about losing him now than ever. She wondered why it had to be. It just was not fair—she had been alone so much of her life! She was so blue and almost in tears, this gloomy cheerless day, when suddenly she raised her head to listen, for her beloved husband was talking to her, in to her mind, plainly, clearly, unmistakably, "Alice, dear, I want you to know that I am sorry that I had to leave you."

Now, she was comforted, for she felt more secure to realize that the bands of death do not cut off all communication. She could see the day of their reunion sometime in the future and the realization brought tears of joy to her heart and eased the burden there. She soon began to mend and to accept her loss, and to learn to make a new and different kind of life for herself and family.

A Departed Son Sends Word to His Mother

In the summer of 1972 a great tragedy befell Sister Olive Bown of Bountiful, Utah. Her beloved son, Mike, who drove a bread truck, was shot and killed in a grocery store hold-up, along with one other person. A third person escaped death because the gun misfired. Mike was always a special and helpful son to her because he showed so much concern for her well-being and was pleased with her activity with the youth of the church. Following his death her grief was sad to see. She found it terribly difficult to accept the loss of this very special son. Her husband and family and the young friends she worked with in church tried to console her and tell her that Mike would not want her to feel so desolate and heartbroken. Despite the help and comfort they gave her, acceptance of her loss was slow to come.

Soon after he died, a young lady who had been dating Mike came to her with the following story: Mike had come to her, after his death, with a message for his mother. He said to tell her that he was alright and beg her not to grieve so much. The young lady said that as she saw him, she marvelled at the brilliant and luminous white clothing that he was wearing. As she beheld him, she moved forward toward him with outstretched hands. He said to her, "No, you cannot touch me." Then the vision faded and he was gone.

The mother pondered this for days and wondered why her son had not appeared to her instead, to give her comfort. Longing to see her son welled up in her breast.

Shortly after this experience, a neighbor boy and very good friend of Mike's came to tell her that Mike had appeared to him also, and had instructed him to "Tell my Mother that I am happy here. Tell her that Scott (a friend who had died in Vietnam) and I are up here doing missionary work. We are getting along fine."

As the neighbor told this story, again she wondered why her son had not come to see her and she wept. Nevertheless, the words of her son helped penetrate the great misery which shrouded her and she began to see that he loved and cared for her even beyond the veil.

In time, she began to reassess her life, to accept her loss and today she can say, "Looking back and remembering how I felt because Mike had not come to me, I believe that I might have been more distressed at seeing him, in realizing my loss more fully. Now, I think it was better that he appeared to others and sent the message to me in this way. I know that it did help me to accept his death, knowing that he was happy in his missionary work and that he wanted me to accept his death peacefully."

A Blessing From Beyond the Veil

Seventeen-year-old Jesse Coombs, who lived with his widowed mother in Fairview, Utah, was starting his last year of high school in September, 1945. His mother had been ill for several years with a serious heart condition which had limited his activities greatly. Of late, her illness had worsened until she was bedridden. At times she was quite discouraged, but Jesse tried to ease her burden by taking over the household chores as best he could.

One afternoon as he returned from school, she called him to her side and eagerly told him that she had had a marvelous experience. As he listened, she told him that both his father and her own father had appeared to her and laid their hands on her head to give her a silent blessing.

"What could that mean, Mother?" he asked, "Are you sure that you didn't just dream that they came?"

"Oh, no, Son, I was wide awake, just like I am now, as I am talking to you." She pointed to the wall and continued, "They came through the wall right there and after the blessing, they went through the front windows."

She was so certain, so sure, that he began to believe that it must have been so, and following her death a week later, he could easily accept the reality of the visitation of his father and grandfather. He felt sure that it was a sort of preparation for his mother, so that she would be ready when she was called home.

Grandmothers Return to See Their Families

When I was a small child my Mother's family gathered on her birthday, April 4, 1923, to have lunch and enjoy each other's company. Since it was a large family there was a big group around our dining table. I remember the chatter and laughter as I went into our front hall. As I entered the hall, I looked very intently at a figure in white standing at the double sliding doors that separated the dining room from my parent's bedroom. It was made known to me at that time that this was the grandmother I had never seen who was here watching her family enjoy this party. She turned then, saw me watching her, and slowly faded out of sight as she moved back. I have thought about my precious grandmother many times since then. I feel privileged to have seen her and to have felt the great love she has for her family. This happened at our home in Salt Lake City, Utah.

A similar incident happened to my then-tiny grandson, Robert Lee, who was living in Virginia with his family at the time that my darling mother, Pininah Poole, passed away. A day or so after her death, that spring of 1967, he asked his mother innocently if all dead people wore white. His mother said she thought they did and asked him why he wanted to know. He said, "Oh, I just wondered, because Grandma Poole was dressed in white when she came to see us." Then my daughter asked him when she had come and what had been said. He replied that she hadn't said anything, but had just watched the children playing in their room. I feel that my mother may also have visited my second daughter's family in California before she went "home". She and I had always agreed that it takes more than miles to separate people who love each other as much as we did.

Kay Jacobsen

Her Sister Came to Summon Her

For several years, 16 year-old Joann Pearson had had nephritis. Slowly it moved into the critical stage, despite treatment and care. Her parents owned a ranch in Cornish, Utah and when the day came in 1950 they had to leave home and take Joann to nearby Logan to the hospital, no one felt very hopeful that she would recover, though they prayed that she might find some measure of relief and in some way begin to get better.

Special care and treatment were given to her, but after nearly three weeks, she had become very weak and didn't seem to be making any improvement. One day while some of the family were visiting with her she started up and said, as she gazed into a corner of the room, "Oh, hello, Leona, what are you doing here?" Leona was her sister who had died nearly four years earlier. She had been walking down the street in Logan one day, a young lady of nineteen years of age, when suddenly she was stricken and fainted away. She was pronounced dead at the hospital and it was found that she had had a cerebral hemorrhage which had taken her life instantly.

A second time, Joann spoke to Leona, asking what she was doing there, and then asked the family members if they could not see her. When they said they could not see Leona, Joann said, "Leona wants to take my hand." Soon afterwards she passed away very peacefully. There was no doubt in anyone's mind that she had taken Leona's hand and moved forward into that sweet, peaceful, happy place, the spirit world.

She Saw Her in the Temple

Grace Fillerup, who reached the lively age of 87 in 1975, was in the temple when she became aware that her husband's first wife was standing gazing at her. She looked at her several times; they smiled at each other and seemed to have a special rapport between them.

Sister Fillerup is a very special lady. At the age of 75 years, while waiting for a mission call, her Stake President, who was checking to see why her call hadn't come through was asked, "Do you know how old she is?" He answered with, "Yes, and you'd better hurry up and call her on a mission or she'll join the Peace Corps." She did fulfill a mission at that age. Presently she is engaged in many projects, one of which is working on her 17th journal of her life experiences! Yes, in the temple, she knew very well who she saw!

Mother Bids Farewell

In October 1963, Sister Beverly Blundell and other members of her family were saddened by the death of their mother. She had been stricken at home and taken to the hospital, where she was pronounced dead. Sister Blundell and one of her sisters returned to the family home to sit and talk and to think about their beloved mother and of the changes her going would bring about.

As they sat in the living room, scarcely more than an hour and a half after their mother's passing, they both became strongly aware of a presence in the room. They felt a movement as though someone were brushing by them, and also heard a rustling, whooshing, sound. They both knew that it was their mother's spirit, that this was a sort of leave-taking, and they were comforted. One of them spoke about it later, "We knew it wasn't just a breeze, because the air was perfectly still about us. Besides we both had a very strong awareness of Mother's presence." They felt a special closeness to their mother and a warm thankfulness to the Lord for this experience.

She Sees an Unborn Baby as Death Approaches

Acting as a good neighbor and loving sister in the gospel, Sister Helen Bingham, in her capacity as a nurse, had been giving pain-killing shots to Sister S-----, a member of the same ward in Bountiful, Utah. Sister S----- was very close to death after months of suffering with cancer. Sister Bingham, at this time, was five months pregnant. One day as Sister Bingham tried to move her, preparatory to giving her the shot, Sister S----- glanced up and said, "Please be careful, Helen, I don't want you to hurt your baby. I can see him, he looks like your other children and he has big brown eyes. I feel like he is part mine." Three days later Sister S----- passed away.

Four months later in the spring of 1971 a brown-eyed baby boy was born to Sister Bingham and he did indeed look like her other children. This was always a testimony to her of the nearness of the spirit world, which is especially close to those who are so near to passing over into it.

The Child's Spirit Left as She Observed

LaRee Clark Doxey had a time of sorrow, which she looked back upon with sadness. But she was able to see that she had gained several things from the experience: first, an acceptance of the Lord's will, knowing that he is always right; second, patience and fortitude, which prepared her for future times of sorrow; and third, knowledge that unhappy experiences are not always as great a tragedy as they seem at the time. This is her story.

As a very young bride, she was joyfully anticipating the advent of her first child and was looking forward to welcoming this tiny baby into their hearts and home. Unfortunately, the beautiful son born to them was three months premature and was having such a difficult time that the attending doctor said he could not possibly live more than a few hours. Today, this small infant's life could have been sustained by advanced medical know-how and equipment, but at that time, 1924, in Brigham City, Utah, he wasn't given much chance to survive.

This dear sister was so fearful that she would lose her son when he was born that she prayed for the Lord to spare his life and anxiously kept a mother's watch over him, moment by moment, fervently willing him to live. Oh, she could not bear the agony of losing this beloved little spirit and she continued to plead with the Lord as the hours went on. Finally, one day had passed by and he still lived.

He had developed a jaundice condition and only barely held on to life. As she continued the vigil to keep her son, she began to think of the child's struggle to survive. Doubts crept into her mind as whether it was right to hold so tightly to him when he was having such a difficult time. Still, she could not bear the thought of going on without him, so her fervent prayers continued. After a week, he was still alive. The doctor marvelled, yet knew how tenuous was the babe's hold on life. On that day, this sister asked herself if it was right to cling to this tiny infant when he seemed to have such a struggle to live. If God in his wisdom felt it were better that he take this sweet spirit back to him, did she have the right to demand otherwise?

As she entertained these thoughts, there came an almost imperceptible lessening of the tension and agony in her breast. She offered her tearful prayer: "Dear Father in Heaven, if I am wrong in struggling so hard to keep my baby here and thou in thy wisdom know that it is not best, then I am willing to accept thy will; with thy help. In the name of Jesus Christ, Amen."

Relief and misery battled with her spirit and she wept as she opened her eyes and looked toward the tiny cradle where her precious infant lay. Then, as she watched, a white-robed personage entered the room from her right. He moved across the room to the cradle. From that small bed there arose the child's spirit, adult size, and joined the waiting personage and departed from the room.

Shortly thereafter, her husband's father came into the room. He looked at the infant, then hurriedly left the room to confer with his son, saying that the baby had returned to his Father in Heaven. They decided not to tell her until morning, both unaware that she knew.

Although the following time was a sad and difficult one, she took up the threads of her life and in due time had four little spirits come to her, but not without further tragedy, for her last little son also lived but a few days. Although she has had these sorrows, acceptance of the Lord's decisions has left her with peace and tranquility and a sure knowledge that her Father in Heaven has her best interests at heart. Now she can see that those two sons who sojourn in the spirit world have been spared many trials and tribulations.

A Deceased Husband Shows His Concern

In October 1967, three years after they had been divorced, Sister R.M. Thompson's ex-husband passed away. Theirs had been a stormy marriage because he had been an alcoholic who treated her very roughly when he had been drinking. When he was sober, however, he had been a considerate person, remembering holidays with gifts and kindnesses. He was a man of strong passions and high temper who was determined to have his own way, which may have contributed to his drinking problem. At last she had left him, filed for divorce and started a new life for herself and children.

At the time of his death she was unhappy because she could not yet forgive him, but still felt aggrieved at the treatment she had received at his hands. After about four months, in February, 1968, she had a strange dream in which she saw him. In her dream she was standing outside her home when she saw her husband enter the front door. She hastened to follow him through the open door and stayed close to the wall as she moved into the room. Although she was deathly afraid she spoke to him, saying, "You shouldn't be here, you're dead." He said to her in a sweet, gentle way, "I just wanted to know how you are. I was concerned about you."

He then moved out through the door and seemed to leave. She stood in the living room as a peaceful and relaxed feeling came over her. When she awakened, however, she was very disturbed, wondering just what the dream meant. While she was thinking about the dream, a vision opened before her eyes and she saw a huge set of iron gates about twenty feet high and fifteen feet wide which clanged twice, then stood ajar revealing an exceedingly bright light streaming from beyond. Outside the gates, on a rounded, smooth surface which appeared to be made of metal, kneeled her ex-husband dressed in white pants and shirt with his dark head bowed slightly. Nearby stood a gloriously white-clad personage with outstretched hands, palms down, which were extended over her husband's head. This figure seemed to be slightly elevated above the kneeling figure and did not touch him with his outstretched hands. The personage raised his head to look at her, yet no words were spoken. As she remained watching, she noted that the scene before her had a dark aura around it which acted as a background, but the depth of the doors and the extent of the light beyond was not determinable. Suddenly she received an intense feeling of peace and acceptance, a feeling of being cleansed. As the scene faded she leaned back on her pillows to think about the vision she had been blessed to see. The dream and the vision—could they mean that he wanted his temple work done and that she was the one to do it? Well, she would do this for him, get his endowments and see that he was sealed to his parents. Having made this decision she drifted off to sleep once more, at peace with herself at last.

True to her resolve, she followed through and had the sacred ordinances performed for him, but later found she was still harboring resentment and bitterness toward him. Disconcerted, she prayed for help and the thought flashed across her mind, to be forgiven, you have to forgive. To hold a grudge is the greater sin. The thought struck her like a bolt of lightning and she knew she had to forgive him, for her sin was greater than his. From then on she felt at peace because she freely forgave him and wished him well in her heart and mind.

His Loved Ones Visited Him as Death Approached

Brother Iven Burton of Providence, Utah suffered from rheumatoid arthritis, a condition which became more severe as the years rolled on and eventually was complicated by a heart problem. He was nearing seventy in the spring of 1964 and the severity of his arthritis was causing him almost continual pain, which they were trying to help by carefully controlled medication.

One afternoon while his wife, Florence, was working in the kitchen, she heard him call out to her. She hurried toward his room to see what he wanted, "Mother, come and see! Come and say hello to Mother and Aunt Mary. They've come to see us!" He sounded very excited. "Honey, I can't see a soul," she answered. He continued, "Oh, there's so many here now, Mother and Dad and some of my friends, but who is that little short fellow?"

His wife looked puzzled and wondered what was going on. Was he really seeing these people? What could it mean? She tried to comfort and calm him.

In less than a week, he passed away. The family realized, upon hearing the story of the visitors from beyond the veil, that his parents and friends and other relatives had come that he might be better prepared for his journey to the spirit world. The family found great comfort in knowing that death, for him, had been a peaceful and happy experience.

Unidentified Knocks when Her Daughter-In-Law Died

Every afternoon at 3:00 p.m., Grandma Kathryn Whitesides of Burley, Idaho used to turn on the television, lie down, and rest while watching it. Her room was near the door into the kitchen and also near to the back door, which was the main entrance to her home, through long use and practice. In her small town, everyone who visited her dropped in at the back door. Perhaps that is why she was surprised when she heard a sharp rapping at her front door. "Now that's strange." she thought, but hastened to the front door, wondering who her visitor might be. No one was there! She then wondered if they might have gone around to the back door, so she hurried there, expecting a knock momentarily. She swung the door open to discover an empty stoop—no one was there either! "That's mighty strange," she thought again, but shrugging her shoulders at the unexplainable and went back to watch T.V. again.

Almost as soon as she relaxed on the bedspread, she heard a loud knocking, this time at the back door. However, no one was there, nor could she hear retreating footsteps or any other sound. She pondered about it and finally said to herself, "I think I am being told something or am being prepared for something. I think it must be a warning of some kind."

That evening, she received a telegram at nine o'clock to say that her beloved daughter-in-law had been killed in an automobile accident at three o'clock—just at the time of her mysterious knocks. Now she knew that it was a leave-taking—an acknowledgment that her loved one was departing this life and it helped to ease the sorrow in her heart that evening in 1963.

They Learned They Should Raise Their Daughter's Child

It happened on Sunday, January 14, 1963 about 4:30 a.m. I was awakened by a rather tall woman dressed in an old-fashioned dress. She was standing at the foot of my bed with a friendly smile on her face. She seemed anxious to tell me something and the moment I looked at her she began talking to me, "I am your sister and I have something to tell you, it is very important." I turned my head away from her and hoped she would leave as it seemed I was fighting off hearing what she had to say. I was not afraid of her, but just was not intending to listen. I covered up my head and refused to have anything to do with her.

Again I was awakened by a rustle of skirts coming down the hall and into the bedroom. This time she paused by my husband's side of the bed and spoke to him saying, "I am her sister, and I have something I must tell her. Please ask her to listen, it is very important." He turned over to me and smiled but did not speak. She leaned over him, reached down and took hold of my hand and I felt it to be real. She was smiling as she said, "I want to tell you that your daughter is going to have a baby and this baby is going to be a *very special person* in your life. I want you to listen to me for this is very important that you should know this." At that, she left and I could still feel the warmth of her hand in mine.

The next day, late in the afternoon, I asked my fifteen-year-old unmarried daughter if there was any chance that she might be pregnant and she said yes. We started having tests made, which verified this to be so. My husband and I discussed the situation and acknowledged with tears in our eyes that if this was happening to us, there must be some special reason for it. We both agreed that it would be impossible for us to give up this baby that was to become our responsibility.

The doctor assured us that we would be wrong to keep the baby, saying that he could give it a much better education than we could, and also that our daughter would return back to normal much quicker if she never saw the baby. Upon questioning her, we knew that she would not be happy knowing she had lost her baby completely, so we chose to keep the child when it was born and know that the Lord must have had a reason for wanting us to raise that sweet little one.

Her Mother Appeared as a Younger Woman

Rosella S. McDonald of Salt Lake City, Utah, passed away the end of March 1946, after being ill for some time. Soon afterwards, she appeared to her daughter, Grace Fillerup. Her daughter was amazed to note that her mother's snowy white hair was now a dark brown and she appeared to be about 35 years of age. This sweet mother, who was a regal 5' 8" tall, smiled at her daughter and said to her, "I am so very anxious to get at the work." Then she moved away and out of her sight. What a happy experience it was for Grace to see her beloved mother as she looked now, in the spirit world. Sister Fillerup thanked the Lord then and always for the bounteous blessing that he gave to her.

A Young Man Sees Spirit Visitors

In 1972, after long years of struggling to place his feet on the path to the truth and sometimes being deceived by various religious philosophies, a young man decided that he was a failure in life's battles and decided to end his life. After taking an overdose of aspirin, he talked to a lady at the suicide prevention center who was a Latter-day Saint. He could then see that what he had done was wrong and he promptly went to a nearby hospital and had his stomach pumped. Soon after this he left the hospital, unauthorized, and returned to his apartment. Unfortunately he had ingested too much medication and after a restless night in a coma state was discovered by his landlady and taken to a Salt Lake City, Utah hospital where he soon passed away.

His funeral was scheduled in his home ward. At the viewing, prior to the services his younger brother, then aged 13, was sitting opposite the casket. There he experienced a special vision which he accepted without apprehension. He gazed upon two figures who stood in the air at the foot of the casket. He saw the taller (or higher) one reach both hands down to grasp the hands of the other as if to comfort him. He related later to his mother that the figures were only seen from the knees up and that they were hazy and indistinct so he could not recognize the features of either one. At the funeral which followed, his elder brother who was one of the speakers said, "I'm sure that my brother and my father are here today." And at this point the 13-year-old youth thought, "Oh, that's who it was," and he felt sure that he was right. That evening he related the story to his mother and explained in detail all he had observed. His sister later asked why he should be given this experience. The mother answered, "Probably because he is an especially accepting and trusting person." With a loving heart, she felt that she had gained special insights into the feelings of her son who had died and could see that it was a difficult time for him also.

His Mother's Spirit Beckons

Jackie Henderson tells this story: It was in April 1962, in Burley, Idaho, when my Grandmother Kathryn Whitesides was 85 years old and grandfather was 93 that my grandfather, who was sitting in the living room called out excitedly, "Honey, come in here. It's my Mother. I see her face in the T.V." She hurried from the kitchen to see what he was calling her for and he said, "Look, see her face, it's my mother!" and he stopped as grandma said, "I don't see a thing but the black tube."

"Well, it's gone now, but I did see her," he explained. Grandma was kind of skeptical and went back to fixing dinner for them.

A few nights later, he called her again, this time saying, "Come and see, I just looked up at the lamp and I can see Mother's face smiling at me through the lampshade." When Grandma came into the living room, she couldn't see a thing and said, "Oh, you must have imagined it, because there's not a thing there."

"No, I didn't imagine it. She was there just as plain as can be. I know I saw her."

Two days later Grandfather passed away. Grandmother chided herself for not having the perception to realize what was happening. She said, "I should have known that his mother was there to give him warning that he was going to die and that we should be prepared." Scolding herself further, "I should have known it meant that he was going to go, but I tried to talk him out of it. He knew he had seen his mother and I know that he did too."

She Sees Her Son in Two Different Manifestations

On August 8, 1952, my eldest son, Ivan Bryson Jr., then 16 years old, was killed at 4:00 p.m. on a road leading to Bryce Canyon, Utah. He was with a group of boy scouts and three men. They had been traveling in a truck to the canyon and there were more than twenty boys in the back. He had climbed out of the back, hoping to ride up front with the men and was running along the side of the moving vehicle. He turned to jump up on the running-board when his foot slipped and he fell under the wheels.

When the news reached me, it was by way of a telephone call to our home in Bountiful, Utah. The police officer who made the call told me that my son had been killed but failed to tell me the details of the accident. At first he didn't know I had two sons on the trip and I had to wait while he found out which one had been killed. Those few seconds when I waited to hear the name that the police officer would tell me will live forever in my memory as being beyond what can be borne.

The next few hours was spent in calling my husband and also my brother. I knew that neither my husband nor I would be in condition to drive to Richfield, Utah to the mortuary where my son's body had been taken. In those five or six hours, I was only aware of one idea: that I would no longer believe in a God if I could never again look on my son's face. I *did* look again on the face of my beloved son, and it bore no mark of pain, suffering or injury.

My life at this point became a terrible nightmare. My burden had been too heavy and my spirit was unable to endure the pain. I even thought of my own death with longing desire. The only peace in all that agony of pain was when I was on my knees in prayer. But instead of asking for the strength to bear what I had to, I prayed for a chance to see my son again. Even though all reason told me that this was impossible, my yearning heart would not believe.

Seven months later, I had a dream that I was hanging clothes on the clothesline in my back yard. I knew that I was going to need to go to the hospital to have a baby and so I rushed into the house to get my things ready. As I entered my bedroom, Ivan Jr. was lying there. He sat up and looked at me very clearly. He was younger appearing than at the time of his death. I said to him, "So you've come back?" and he answered, "Yes."

"But you'll leave me again," I said.

"I'll *never* leave you again," he stated.

As the months went by, a new understanding seemed to be emerging to explain the dream. I found that I was pregnant, and must have been at the time of the dream. It was almost inevitable that I would put the interpretation on the events surrounding the dream that I did. Since I knew that Ivan was dead and since he told me in the dream that he would never leave me again, then it had to follow that I would die at the time my baby was born. As the months passed, I became more and more convinced that this was what would happen.

When I became very ill a couple of weeks before my baby was due, I was not at all surprised. My husband called the elders to administer to me because he was terribly worried about my attitude. Their blessing that night was the first step in the events that followed when the heavens were opened to me and I saw my son.

I was lying asleep in my bed when an evil power seemed to press down on me, so that I felt that it would kill me. I cried out to my husband, "Ivan"... and "Don't... you're killing me." The pain of the evil pressure left me, and a peaceful feeling took its place. I arose from my bed and walked into an adjoining hall. My surroundings were very clear to me and I was able to observe every detail, even the paper on the walls.

At the entrance to the hall I saw a glorious being. I knew that I was looking at my son, Ivan, but I knew it only by the spirit. I had never before in this life seen anyone with the slightest resemblance to that god-like vision. He appeared very tall, and stood with an erect, kingly bearing. He possessed a radiance and a beauty not of this earth. He did not speak, but only walked toward me, and as he reached me, my senses departed, and I felt myself falling. Arms went around me and when I regained consciousness I was in my own bed.

Even though I have told myself many times throughout the years that this was only a miraculous dream, the inescapable fact remains that no one could have imagined the being that I saw. The difference between the two manifestations that I had was that in the dream Ivan Jr. appeared as I had known him during his lifetime, but in the visitation, he appeared as a glorified being. I know without a doubt that my Father in Heaven *did* answer my prayer at that time and allowed my son to return to me for a few moments to give me the strength I needed so desperately. Who could ever hope for an answer to a prayer such as this? Truly, God lives, and answers the righteous prayers of our hearts.

Violet Bryson

Her Mother Had Been with Her Deceased Family Members

My grandmother died in 1853 while they were crossing the plains on their way to Utah. This left my 17-year-old mother to care for her brothers and sisters, a family of six younger children ranging in age from eighteen months to fifteen years. She told us that her mother appeared to her soon after her death and gave her courage and comfort. She was lying in the wagon on the bedding at noontime, waiting for the company to start, when it happened.

Her mother appeared to her and told her not to feel so badly about her death but to cheer up and to be happy. Mother asked grandmother if Foster, the older brother who had died with fever, was with her. She said that he had been, but had gone to hear the prophet Joseph preach. She also said her brother, Abraham, had been with her too. Mother said when the wagon started up, her mother disappeared.

Later when the youngest child, Agnes, who had been eighteen months old at her mother's death, was about six years old, she told her sister, Sara, that her Mother had come to see her several times when she was out at play.

"What did Mother say to you?" asked Sara.

"Oh, she never said anything, she just looked like she wanted me to come with her. And I am going to go, too."

It was only a very short time until Agnes was accidently shot with a heavy charge of buckshot and passed away from the injuries.

Maggie Tolman Porter

A Visit Each Year on Their Anniversary

My story began eleven years ago, so you see it's a kind of ongoing miracle—but let me tell you more. When I was widowed for a year and our wedding anniversary was approaching, I had made arrangements to go to a symphony concert at the Tabernacle in Salt Lake City, Utah. That evening, November 13, 1965, as I sat enjoying the wonderful music, I suddenly started what I thought was fantasizing. I thought I was talking, in my mind, to my beloved husband and listening to him saying how much he missed me. Then he said that he had been given permission to talk to me each year on our wedding anniversary. I thought it was delightful! This conversation went on after I arrived home, though I still wondered if I was making it all up. It was very pleasant and reminded me how very much I loved and missed my dear companion.

The next year on November 13, 1966, I did not accept this "fantasizing" so easily and I began to argue with myself saying, "Oh, I'm making all this up." Whereupon he would say to me, "No, you are not, I am really here. As I told you, I have been given permission to talk to you each year on our wedding anniversary." Oh, this was very strange, and I wondered why I kept talking to him and occasionally would say, "Oh, I'm making this up," which was followed by his same denial. Afterwards I shook my head and was puzzled, thinking, "Why did I make all this up and why does it seem so real?"

The next year the conversation which he began and which I continued to challenge finally brought a statement from him which hauled me up short. "I might as well not come, if all we are going to do is argue. I have so much work to do that I can't waste my time." I immediately desisted with the denials and began to talk with him because a great fear had come upon me. I thought, "If this *is* real and Father has given me this blessing and I cannot accept it through lack of faith, and then he takes it away from me.... Oh, I cannot take the chance of that happening!" It was very sobering to me and I began to recognize that it was indeed true, and it was a blessing that I wanted to hold onto at all costs. You can guess that I never again did doubt him.

Do you wonder that I found it so hard to accept this visit as a fact, or that I kept it to myself for some time? I couldn't

expect anyone else to believe it, since I had found it so difficult to accept myself. It took a lot of faith to accept and know
that it was actually happening and I was talking to my
husband.

Each year as he has returned to talk with me, I have
learned something new. Once I found out that he couldn't see
me any more than I could see him. I had thought that he could
see me. Just two years ago, I found out that I could initiate
the conversation, whereas before I had always waited for him
to contact me. He had told me that he has seen our
grandchildren several times before they were born and
expressed an opinion about each one, which as you can guess,
is a great delight to our family. Just once, he thought I was
doubting again (it was not so, just a misunderstanding), and
he quickly said to me, "Oh, no, don't start that again, I had
enough trouble with you the first couple of years that I
came." Then he suggested, "I'll tell you what you can do, you
call for me tomorrow and of course I won't answer, then you
try and figure out what I might say and I think you'll be able
to see the difference."

Just as an experiment, I did just that the next day, and
found it was as different as day and night, because I had to
"figure out" what he might be answering especially when I
asked questions where the answer was not known to me.
There was not the spontaneity of a conversation, like the ones
I had been having with him each year, so it only strengthened
my already strong acceptance of this beautiful and special
boon, that the Lord, in his generosity, had been allowing me.

I have found out from my husband that he sometimes is
involved in our lives, perhaps infrequently, for it has been at
times such as when the children are married in the temple.
This experience has served to help me know that help comes
from beyond the veil in many ways to give us the guidance,
the protection, and help that we need as we travel life's difficult, but also at times, joyful road. It makes me think of the
23rd Psalm, The Lord truly is my shepherd and I shall not
want, for he maketh me to lie down in green pastures. I have
felt so blest that with all my heart I say, "Oh, what shall I ask
of thy providence more, dear Father in Heaven?"

Norma C. Larsen

Chapter Ten

GOD ALLOWS VISITS
TO THE SPIRIT WORLD

The experiences which are categorized here as "spirit world experiences" are more unusual, and perhaps more striking, because of their unfamiliar nature. One is always tempted to think of such experiences with a little awe and an almost-questioning attitude. Most are associated with near-death experiences. Like visitations, they are harder for some to accept than healings and various answers to prayers, for instance. Why it should be any harder for the Lord to accomplish this type of miracle is a question we have no way of answering, if indeed it be so. If he in his goodness can help us in myriads of other ways, then there is no reason why we should not accept these as certainly within the range of his blessings to his children.

The first story is about a man who had the experience of seeing, while at death's door, his own body lying in a hospital bed and also seeing his ward primary praying for him—an interesting combination of events.

Though Close to Death, He Returns to Life

In November 1955, Bishop Rex L. Tolman of Wyoming, was taken to Salt Lake City for surgery to remove a calcium deposit which had encased his heart. His experiences at that time served to increase his testimony of the gospel, and particularly his faith in the power of prayer. Following is his report and testimony concerning his experiences at that time:

"While on the operating table during the surgery my heart stopped beating. For a period of about an hour circulation was maintained by the massaging of my heart. The doctors reported that at this time there was no indication that the heart would again start to beat without some other stimulation. It was therefore decided to administer electrical shocks. It is apparently normal to administer no more than two shocks, since it is felt that if there are no results with two, there will probably be no results at all. However, on the second shock there was still no response. Feeling there was nothing to lose, they tried a third shock, and the heart began to fibrillate.

"Although there was still some calcium remaining on my heart, the doctors decided to leave it there since the restrictive portion had been removed and they felt it would be dangerous to continue the operation. This surgery lasted seven hours.

"The first thing I recall was when my wife, Dorene, and one of the nurses were standing by my bed telling me how good I felt. I must admit that there were times in my life when I had felt better, so I told them they were bearing false witness against me.

"The periods of time for the next day or two were a little confusing and it is difficult for me to tell any particular sequence for the events that followed.

"I particularly remember that every 20 minutes I would be asked to pull myself up to a sitting position by a strap attached to the foot of the bed. Then Dorene or one of the nurses would hold me around the chest while I tried to cough up any congestion that had formed in my chest.

"We were told that if I should go to sleep within 24 hours after the operation I would probably never wake up. A talkathon by Dorene and our mothers ensued, and I recall that I became very tired of women talking—an affliction from which I have not yet entirely recovered.

"At one time I remember that I felt I was looking down from what seemed to be the east wall of my hospital room and seeing myself lying in the bed. Several times I was sure I could feel myself 'slipping o'er the brink' but Dorene kept talking me out of it. I found out then that death is no tragedy, that the experience of passing from this realm is a happy, pleasant one. Though pain and suffering may precede the actual experience of death, death itself is a glorious feeling, and I wanted so badly to go all the way. Only the continuous encouragement of my wife kept me from doing it.

"I am told that for the first two days there was never a moment when there was not someone by my bedside. There was a time, however, when I felt the spirit of the gospel so strongly that I knew I could convince anyone of its truthfulness just by saying that it was true—and at that time there was no one in the room because I even wished for Satan to enter the room because I felt so strongly I thought I could call him to repentance.

"Probably the greatest experience of them all was on the day following the operation. I had been quite uncomfortable and the pain seemed to be increasing when suddenly I felt myself literally lifted from the bed. I could feel myself about six inches above the hot, sweaty sheets, and the pain seemed to leave my body and remain in the bed. I could see the primary in session in the Burlington Ward Chapel and Max Johnson was giving the prayer. I could hear him saying, 'and bless our Bishop...'. From that moment on I recovered very rapidly. I was soon out of bed and taking care of myself. Interns and medical students were brought in and the case was reviewed for them because of some of its peculiarities. The rapid recovery was surprising, even to the doctors.

"When I had been brought down from the the operating room, Dorene was told that I would probably not live through the night. I know for a surety that the prayers of the people in the Big Horn Stake [Wyo.]—and more especially those of the good people of the Burlington Ward—together with the untiring efforts of my wife and our mothers have combined to save my life. From many experiences but from this one in particular, I know that God answers prayers. I have felt the power of the combined prayers of many people. I have felt that had there been even one less person praying for me, I could not have remained here.

"To this day I am not sure why my life was preserved. Perhaps there is a work yet to be done. I can say this—that I know God lives. I have felt his power through your prayers."

Rex L. Tolman

It Wasn't His Time to Enter the Spirit World

When I was a little girl, my Mother first told me this story, but I have heard it many times since; it is about my Grandfather Robert McCulloch of Logan, Utah. Lots of people were ill, lots of people had died with the dread flu during the big epidemic of 1918. When Grandpa got the flu, everyone was terribly fearful for his well-being.

One day Mother was sitting beside him, taking a turn helping him as she could while the others worked in the garden and fields. He was lying quietly, breathing heavily, when suddenly his breathing ceased. Frightened, Mother ran out into the garden to get Grandma and to tell her that Grandpa had died. They hurried back to his side and as they gazed at him, suddenly his breathing resumed and he opened his eyes, looked puzzled for a moment, then became very animated as if realizing he was still alive. "Oh, Mother," he choked out, "I've been to the most beautiful place, where everyone is so happy and so kind and loving. He stopped then, and a look of almost sadness moved across his face, "Oh, I so much wanted to stay there, it was a wonderful place and everyone was full of love for others."

Grandma said to him, "You must have gone to the spirit world, dear. Did you see your mother and father?"

"Oh, yes, and lots of other relatives and friends too. They said to me, 'Oh, what are you doing here? It isn't your time to come yet.' I hated to leave. I wished I didn't have to go. I'll never forget that beautiful place."

Grandpa recovered from the flu and lived for many years before he once again had his chance to go to the spirit world, that place he thought so very beautiful and joyous. We have always thought that this was a wonderful experience he had, and we knew that he lived so that he could return to "heaven" as he expressed it.

Experiences While Searching for the True Church

After she reached the age of twenty in the summer of 1971, Jane Holmstrom talked to Sue, her best girlfriend, about religion. Since she had been raised in a religious family, she was no stranger to the subject, and neither was Sue. Ofttimes they had talked about religion even though they had not attended a church regularly. They felt they wanted to know more on the subject. A longing to know if there was anything they were missing, if there was one true church, encouraged them to keep seeking.

Sue called Jane one evening and said to her, "Members of the Jehovah Witnesses came by while I was at work and left some pamphlets. Shall we contact them and start a search in earnest?"

Jane agreed and that turned out to be the beginning of their search for a true church. They soon moved along to other churches and Sue affiliated with "Good News" Groups who were seeking to learn more about Jesus and his life. Jane didn't join in but wanted to keep looking elsewhere.

While they were investigating churches and reading pamphlets, Jane had several unhappy experiences. Later she had one very wonderful experience also. The first one that happened, she could only think of as an evil power manifestation which she recalls in this way, "I was lying on the bed one evening reading the Bible when I began to reflect about religion and put the book aside for a moment. Suddenly I felt a strong weight pressing down on my chest and body, almost as though a spirit was trying to move right in with me. I fought and struggled with all my strenth to force it off or out. It was so overpowering that I could hardly breathe and my speech was slurred and choked as I tried to call for help. My sister said I just gurgled and that strangled sounds were all that came out. 'Please dear Lord, help me,' I prayed in my mind over and over. All the while I was pushing and struggling to force the evil thing away, to keep it from suffocating me. It wasn't for very long, but it just seemed like a long time because I was so scared. Suddenly it moved away and the hateful, fearful feeling in the room was gone. This same experience occurred four other times in the six months we were investigating churches. I finally decided it must be some kind of evil spirit and told my mother about it. She, at first thought that I had imagined it, but when it happened a second time, she was alarmed too."

Near the end of the year that she and Sue had begun their search for a true church, she had a very different and beautiful experience. One evening as she was going up to bed, she suddenly found herself running up the stairs with a happy anticipation that something special was going to happen and hurriedly climbed into bed. She tells of her experience in this way, "The second that I lay down on the bed I suddenly felt lifted up and felt a sort of floating weightlessness come over me. A delightful, happy feeling accompanied this airiness, and as I looked down I saw my body lying on the bed. At first, I thought I must be dead. I said to myself, 'So this is what it feels like to be dead'. I felt so free and peaceful and totally without fear. There was a golden glow around me and I was aware that there were others nearby, but felt no compulsion to turn my head and look at them. After what seemed like just a few minutes I felt a gentle pressure all over me as I was pushed slowly down toward my body. A few seconds later I looked up from my place on the bed and wondered what this experience meant."

After that time, she once again experienced the visitor of evil, as she came to think of it, but she continued to search for the truth, trusting the Lord to help her.

The phone rang one afternoon, and Sue told her excitedly, "The Mormon Missionaries working in the Pittsburg area came by and talked with me. They've invited me out to their church. Would you like to go with me Tuesday night?" Jane answered, "I'd be glad to go."

For three months the missionaries worked with them and they participated in church meetings. Jane didn't know if she could believe the doctrine, but she was so hungry to know the truth that she kept coming, learning and arguing. She told the missionaries, "I really want to know. It's very important to me, but I must be sure." In answer she was told to follow the admonition of Moroni: And when ye shall receive these things, I would exhort you that ye would ask God, the eternal Father, in the name of Christ, if these things are not true: and if ye shall ask with a sincere heart, with real intent, having faith in Christ, He will manifest the truth of it unto you, by the power of the Holy Ghost. And by the power of the Holy Ghost ye may know the truth of all things.

These words touched her heart and she resolved to heed them and the words of the missionaries who told her she would have to find out for herself by praying and asking specific questions of the Lord.

She read from the Bible, put the book down and humbly beseeched her Father in Heaven to tell her if the church was true and if Joseph Smith was a prophet. She told the Lord that she was hungry to know the truth and that it was terribly important to her. Emotion-filled, she waited, and very soon she was literally filled with the spirit—it was great joy, peace and happiness with a strong knowledge flooding her being. "I just *knew* it was true," she said later, "I was not confused any more and there was no feeling of doubt. It all fit together, like pieces of a jig-saw puzzle; it just fell into place and I was elated."

Both she and Sue joined the church and today Jane is married to a good Latter-day Saint, in the temple, and is the mother of a baby son. Her Mother and three sisters have followed her into the church and she says, "For our memberships I am most humbly grateful."

She Was Not Permitted to Enter the Door

During the birth of Lucille Clark's fourth child on November 20, 1931 complications arose. The doctor had pushed the baby upward in an effort to help it turn properly into the birth channel. Sister Clark began sinking fast, and soon became oblivious to her surroundings. Her vital signs showed she was expiring.

At this point, she became conscious of her deceased grandmother who was standing in a small room looking at her. Nearby was a door upon which Sister Clark fixed her attention. Her Grandmother, who in life spoke no language but Dutch, spoke to her in English and said, "You have come too soon and you must go back." Sister Clark said to her, "No, Grandmother, I want to see Daddy Clark." He was her husband's long-deceased father. "I've never met him and always wanted to see him. Is he there through that door?" Her Grandmother answered, "Yes, he is, but you cannot go through that door because you then could not go back. You are still needed there to raise your family." At this, Sister Clark moved toward the door. Her grandmother went quickly to bar her way through the doorway. At this point, she heard a voice far off in the distance calling her to come back; it was her husband pleading with her to come back and help him raise the children.

As she returned to consciousness and listened to her husband, she was told that the doctor had called him into the room saying, "Your wife is gone and you'd better come and call her back." It was at that moment that she had heard her husband's voice pleading with her to return. She told him of her experience and lamented, "I never did get to see Daddy Clark." Then she told him of seeing her grandmother and ended by saying, "I felt bad because I didn't get to meet your father. I had always heard so many stories about what a wonderful person he was." He nodded his head and commented, "Oh, that's why it took you so long to come back."

They were always grateful that she had been permitted to return to him and to their family.

She Saw Flowers Beyond the Veil

In 1931 Sister Loy Spencer, of Roy, Utah, was very ill with cancer. The disease had progressed until she was terribly weak and in great pain. At this point in her illness she had the following experience: An evil spirit, which she believed to be Satan, put a knife in her hand, as though to suggest that she take her own life. She struggled, fought, and refused to grasp the knife. She thought to herself, "How strong he is, and how strong is the power he has over you, especially when you are so weak, so weak." She prayed for help and soon the evil presence left.

Not long after this she grew so ill that she passed into a coma and went for a short time into the spirit world. When she returned to her body and consciousness, she told her family that she had been in the most wonderful place—the flowers were everywhere and were fantastically beautiful, far beyond any they had ever seen. She had always loved flowers and worked in her garden many long hours to make it a lovely spot to visit. Her eyes seemed to sparkle as she pictured the beauty of that heavenly garden she had seen. She continued, "While I was there I saw my little baby sister. She was not a baby any more, she was all grown up."

Sister Spencer continued to grow weaker and weaker following this incident and within a few days she passed away. Her story has been told within their family for many years and has proved a source of gratitude for the Lord's promise of a beautiful life after death.

Her Guardian Angel Showed Her

An experience which I hold very sacred happened to me at my home, 127 Vidas Avenue in Salt Lake City on August 5th, 1928. When I returned home after working at a root beer stand at 12:15, the words of the song, "Have I Done Any Good in the World Today?" ran through my mind and I strongly felt the spirit of the Lord with me as I knelt to pray. Never have I felt so humble and close to my Heavenly Father! I really prayed with all my heart and soul.

I no sooner rose and got settled in bed than I heard a voice call "Ruby." I thought it must have been my sister Elma, so I went to her room and asked if she had called me. She told me she hadn't so I woke my sister Katherine and she too said she had not called me. Feeling somewhat frightened, I went back to bed. No sooner was I settled down than I heard my name called again. I was puzzled and troubled, because I knew that the voice had come from somewhere in the house, so I got up enough courage to wake my parents and ask them; mother had been working hard and was very tired, but they both said no. When my brother also said "No." to me, I was concerned, but went to bed, knowing that I had heard my name called twice.

As soon as I was once more settled in bed, I again heard a voice call "Ruby." and this time it seemed close by and I could feel a presence in the room. Then I saw a beautiful girl, who appeared to be between 23 and 25 years of age, standing beside me. She was wearing a long white dress and she smiled as she said, "Ruby, come with me." She said no more and then I knew I had left my body, and I followed her. I glanced back to see my body in the bed as we left the room and started down the street a half-block to State Street. When we arrived there the veil lifted and I knew I was in a different world— it all happened swifter than lightning—the change, I mean.

I saw a meadow and lots of people. We went up some stairs, and I felt frightened suddenly and the young lady said to me, "Be not afraid, I will always be with you." She then took me further up the stairs, pausing to rest on the landing. I saw Orin Yancy, a recently deceased schoolmate of mine. I wished to speak to him but was told, "No, you have not yet received the key or authority to go where you want to go."

We entered a building that had a large, very long hall, covered with tables at which people were sitting working or conversing. I looked as we passed to see if there was anyone I knew there. At one large table there were two empty chairs. Beside this table was a man who had laid hands on my head when I was doing baptisms for the dead. We passed on and found a place outside where we sat and talked. She told me that she was my guardian angel, and that she had been with me constantly since I came to earth. She instructed me about many other things, including the three degrees of glory. I felt that I should have lived a better life and accomplished more than I had; I voiced this to her and she said that I had nothing to fear, that I had lived well, but I had been a little inclined to judge people.

As I saw others busy and happy, I felt that I wanted to go back and get my temple work done, so I could return and work in the celestial kingdom, so I knelt and prayed for another chance to return to earth. I prayed fervently with all my heart and soul for this petition to be granted. As I rose, I saw in the nearby area, the Savior with a group of people, he looked toward me and raised one of his arms toward me saying, "You may go back and have the privilege of going through the temple. I have heard your prayers."

As we retraced our steps down the stairs I was aware of signs along the way which said, Judge Not That Ye Be Not Judged. We soon returned to my room and when I was once more in my body, I arose and checked the time—it was 9:30 a.m. I asked my sisters and later my parents why no one had awakened me. They all said they had forgotten.

The above story does not include all the things I learned, things about the beauties of this life and the next; but I know that I will strive to live to return there, and strive to always say 'no' to all that is not pure and holy. This experience will always be a shining light in my life; much of it I cannot put in words.

From the Book of Remembrance of Ruby Lee Vaughn

She Asked Not to be Called Back to Mortality

Sister Orpha Orulian of Salt Lake City, Utah had been very ill with leukemia for several years and in 1951 it had reached the critical stage. It was with great regret that her friends and family watched her sink into a near coma state and they wept because she was so terribly ill.

Years before, she had been left a young widow with three children to raise and had worked hard to fulfill her role as mother and breadwinner. After several years of struggling to do the job by herself, she had married a very fine man who loved and cared for her and helped her raise her children.

After her illness progressed still further, the day came when she sank lower and lower and finally passed over into the spirit world. With great grief her husband begged a dear friend of the family, who was with them at this time, to administer to her and ask the Lord to send her back. Brother Lynn McKinley blessed Sister Orulian and pleaded with the Lord for her return to her family.

As the family stood by, prayerfully, Sister Orulian's spirit returned to her body, much to the joy and thankfulness of her husband and children. When she was alone with her daughter, she said to her, "Oh, I didn't want to come back. I saw your father and I was very, very happy. Now, if I go again, don't ever bring me back."

Within a few days she once more sank into a coma and passed away a second time. Although Brother Orulian asked Brother McKinley for a second administration to call her back he was told that usually when a person is brought back and they don't stay very long, it would not be right to ask for her return a second time. Brother Orulian thanked Brother McKinley and sorrowfully accepted his loss.

Her Relatives Gave Her Messages

An early snow storm had covered the ground on Friday, October 1, 1971. My cousin's wife, Carolyn, and her two children, Gregg, four, and Shannon, 10 months, arrived at our home to take me and my one-year-old son, Robert, to the Homecoming assembly in Afton, Wyoming, fifteen miles away.

We had traveled about a mile when the accident occured which took the lives of Carolyn and her two children. I vaguely remember the car starting to skid and the next thing I remember was being in the spirit world. The beauty, peace and happiness that existed there is beyond our earthly imaginations. There were green rolling hills and flowers everywhere. The colors were of a nature that I had never seen before. A happiness that completely filled our beings permeated this beautiful place.

It was there in this beauty and happiness that I saw Carolyn, Gregg and Shannon. Carolyn was holding Gregg and Shannon by the hand and they were running through the flowers. Their beauty and happiness radiated from them and I knew they had been called to do a special work for our Heavenly Father.

The next thing that I remembered was the feeling of traveling very fast, but I cannot remember where it was, nor to whom I listened next, but I was privileged to see eight people I knew. Four of them spoke to me, each one had a message that he wanted delivered:

1. My husband Ron's grandfather, Edward Keeler, told me that he needed his work done and when he said this, many people appeared before me as if they too were waiting for their temple work to be done.

2. Ron's uncle, Ford Nelson, told me how happy he was that his wife, Laura, had remarried and expressed his contentment with the kind of life that she has now. (Aunt Laura has had Uncle Ford sealed to her in the temple and has become active in the church since his death.)

3. My Grandfather, Issac Franklin Dana, told me that he had been working very hard and that he had a few more things to do and then he would be able to cross over. (Grandpa had been inactive while here on earth and we feel that it has taken him this long to accomplish what he could have done here. He died in December 1947.)

4. My Grandfather, Lorenzo Jensen, told me that it wouldn't be long before he would come for Grandma. (Grandma Jensen died October 29, 1974, three years following my visit with grandpa.)

I also saw my Uncle, Roy Dana, Arnold Passey, Carl LeCheminant and DeLoyd Coates: they were all busy and happy. I sensed the feeling of "busyness" and of the time being very short. No one told me that I couldn't stay, but I knew that I was to return, that my work had not been completed.

It was very hard for me to be contented here on earth and for the first few days after this experience, I felt very cheated and unhappy because I was here. I know that someday, when it is my time, that I will again go to this beautiful place if I will but live as I should. I feel that what I saw and felt is just a small part of what our Heavenly Father has prepared for us. I know that our Heavenly Father lives and that he loves each of us very much. I know that Jesus truly is his Son and that he lives and loves us too.

How grateful I am to be a member of the church to have an opportunity for such wonderful blessings that come from being a member of The Church of Jesus Christ of Latter-day Saints. I am so grateful for my wonderful husband and for our four sons; the two youngest have come to our home since the accident. I know that the Church is true, I bear testimony to you that the things which I have written are true, I cannot deny what I experienced, and have no desire to do so. I don't know why I had this great opportunity, but I am indeed grateful for it and hope that it will help others. I bear testimony to you in the name of Jesus Christ, Amen.

Anna Dana Erickson

Chapter Eleven

OTHER FAITH-PROMOTING EXPERIENCES

Following will be four stories, which must be called multi-category because to break them down into individual stories to fit those areas treated to this point, would cause them to lose a great deal of their impact, therefore they follow intact.

A Bishop Receives Inspiration

Bishop Norman Gale of a ward located in Salt Lake City, Utah, a most spiritual and humble man, has attested to receiving inspiration, guidance and many promptings, which he calls receiving a witness", on behalf of members of his ward. He says it is exciting to see the Gospel in the lives of the members and he feels exceedingly blessed that the Lord has given him so many opportunities to help people, especially those in his ward. His stories about members are told with their permission, but names are changed to protect their privacy. These experiences occurred between 1974 and 1976.

* * * * * *

A dear sister in our ward, whom I will call Sister Smith, had been divorced and was raising her family, supporting herself and children by giving piano lessons. Her youngest child, who was a number of years younger than his nearest sibling, had been creating an unhappy situation in the home because he had so many problems. She had called on the school principal, her bishop, and finally on a professional counselor to help her cope with the child's problems and with her own emotional upsets. She had also gone to her father, who was a stake patriarch, and asked for his support and guidance. When he called and asked me to come over one evening and administer to his daughter, I thought it was in reference to the emotional upsets she had been experiencing.

As I arrived, I anticipated that he would ask me to anoint with oil and he would give her the blessing, but he took the oil and held it while he explained to me, "We'd like to tell you the nature of the problem that my daughter has. She has been suffering a hearing loss and although we have been to the best doctors both here and in California, they say that nothing can be done for her and that the loss will become more severe with time. She needs her hearing to continue her work and to support her family as a piano teacher. We'd like you to give her the blessing that the Lord wants her to have."

I was amazed to hear of her problem, but I also was fearful. I was thinking that her father, who was accustomed to giving blessings, and who was a spiritual giant, was the right one to give the blessing to her, so I searched my mind to try and think of anything I might have done that possibly might negate the blessing that the Lord wanted her to have, and could find nothing. I listened with tears in my eyes as Brother Smith performed the anointing. As we held our hands on her head the blessing she received was that the loss of hearing would no longer be of concern to her and that the loss would be retarded and cause her no further trouble the rest of her life. The emotional strain she had been under would also be alleviated and eased for her and she could continue to earn her living as she had done in the past.

When we were through, I went home feeling very good about the blessing and very thankful to the Lord. A few weeks later, after weekly visits to her doctor, Sister Smith reported to me that her doctor said that the hearing loss had ceased, as far as he could see. Later, he was sure that it had cleared up entirely. This was but another evidence that the priesthood steps in where the medical profession cannot and manifests the power of God in our behalf.

* * * * * *

So many times the Lord has given me promptings to know when ward members are in need of help of varying kinds. One time, a beautiful, special young lady, that I shall call Susan, had a serious problem that needed to be resolved, but no one would have suspected it just to look at her. One day I was surprised when the Holy Ghost testified to me that she had need of help to resolve a very serious problem.

I asked her to come into my office for a moment and after telling her of my respect and love for her said, "Susan, it has been revealed to me that you have a serious problem that you need to work out. I don't know what the nature of the problem is, but I would like to help."

She almost wept as she said, "I don't know how you know, but I do have some problems, but I'm not talking to you about them. I've never talked to anyone about them."

"Susan, do you know how much I love you?"

"Yes, Bishop, I know you love me."

"Do you trust me, Susan?" and once more she said "Yes, but I can't discuss it with you." When I explained to her that she really needed help, she agreed but said she just could not tell me about it.

For six months I encouraged her to confide in me and relieve her mind and heart in so doing, but she only said she couldn't because I would lose respect for her if she did. I denied that I would lose respect for her, but it did not help and she reaffirmed her position.

Finally, I kneeled and prayed telling the Lord how much I desired to help Susan and at that time the nature of her problem was revealed to me. Although I had been prompted many times before, that members needed help, this was the first time that the nature of the problem had been given to me. I was strengthened to strive harder to get her to talk to me, but she had many legitimate excuses for not accepting the interview times I tried to set with her. In fact, she seemed greatly relieved that she was unable to keep such an appointment with me.

I persisted, however, and set a future time a week from the next Sunday at 4:00 p.m. In answer to this request, she flatly stated, "Bishop, I refuse an interview with you." and walked out of the office. Later, she apologized for walking out on me, but reaffirmed her refusal to meet with me and at that time I told her that the appointment still stood and I planned to meet with her then.

So strongly did she feel that she wrote on a sheet of paper, "I refuse an interview with you" and held it up under her chin where I could see it when conducting meetings. I

smiled and looked at her as she sat in the first or second row
where no one could see what she was doing, but still intended
to press for the interview.

I was there that Sunday at 5 minutes to 4:00 to be certain
she could not say she had come and I was not there. I waited
hopefully and at four o'clock she came in carrying her sign
and said, "I'm not going to talk with you." I encouraged her,
saying, "Susan, you need help and it will help you to talk with
me and get it out of your system and put it behind you. I know
it is bothering you and that you have even stopped prayer."
"That's true," was her answer, "I don't get answers to my
prayers." I suggested, "You don't like to go to church even."
That brought her retort that "I hate church and only go because my mother makes me."

After one more, "I'm not going to tell you" I said to her,
"I want you to know that I know the nature of your problem,
because the spirit of the Holy Ghost bore witness to me."

"You couldn't know, because I've never told anybody."
then she burst into tears and said, "Bishop, I've known for
two weeks that you knew about my problem." It was my turn
to be surprised, but I listened as she continued, "Just in case
you are trying to get me to tell you by a trick, I want you to
tell me...."

I began, "Point one" and I stated it as she stared at me
open mouthed. "And point two" which I clearly related and
"Point three, which is the worst of all" I added which was
followed by great sobs on her part as she said, "I know that
this has to be the true church because you only have known
these things by revelation. It happened a long time ago in a
different state and I never told anyone."

"Yes, Susan, the Church is true and many times I have
been told when the members have needed help."

"Bishop, will you give me a blessing?" she pleaded, and I
readily and gladly did so, which seemed to relieve her sorrow
a great deal.

Several days later she came to me to say, "I want you to
know that I am a new person. I have been praying to the Lord
and I know that he hears me. I have been so happy that I wish
I had come to you a lot earlier."

She began to enjoy going to church and became very
diligent in studying the scriptures.

* * * * * *

A few years ago, a new couple who I shall call Brother and Sister Jones, moved into our ward. It so happened they moved in just a few doors from our home and I witnessed her joy and pleasure in finding herself in such a warm and friendly neighborhood. We called on them to find that they were pleased and excited to be here, more especially because they had not wanted to move here. It was soon apparent that they had not been very active in the church, but I received a witness that they could be helped and activated once more.

I was acquainted with Brother Jones' brother at the place where I work and one day I asked him if he could tell me something about Brother Jones. He then told me that at one time Brother Jones had been very active in the church and concluded by saying, "The only way he will be reactivated will be by a miracle." I was pleased to tell him, "I'd like you to be aware that I have received a witness from the Lord, that he may be activated once more, so maybe we have that miracle."

As time went on Sister Jones began to attend sacrament meeting, somewhat irregularly, but I was pleased to see her there. One day as I saw her I received a witness that she needed help, so I spoke to her in the foyer and asked, "You need to meet and talk with me, don't you?" Startled, she looked up with tears in her eyes and said, "How did you know?" "Because I have received a witness. Shall we make an appointment to talk?"

She readily agreed and seemed excited and enthused about the forthcoming appointment. Unfortunately I was unable to keep this appointment, and she was very disappointed. However I soon made a new one and met with her for two hours where she told of the transgressions she and her husband had been guilty of. I cautioned her that her husband must be the one to "tell his own sins" and ended by asking her if she wanted a blessing. In part the blessing said, You have been placed on this earth to be an instrument to uplift other spirits, to add dimension to their testimonies and to strengthen them spiritually. She looked up at me and said, "Don't go away, I have something to show you." and she hurried down the hall to a cupboard and returned with her patriarchal blessing and showed me two sentences that said almost word for word the ones in the blessing I had just pronounced on her head. She went on, "I *knew* that the Lord wanted us to be active again. I am so grateful that the Lord reveals to our leaders that we need help because I never could have done this on my own."

As I left I repeated that her husband must come on his own and she must not try to force him. It was about seven months later that he came to me and said, "I know that you know about my problems, because my wife told me she had revealed them to you, but I need to tell you myself."

Today both Brother and Sister Jones are fully active in the church and serve with strength. They both hold temple recommends and he holds positions of trust in the Church. I consider them two of the most spiritual supporters in the ward.

* * * * * *

One Sunday I was involved in a sacrament meeting which was put on by the Primary. It was a once-a-year, special program and was especially good with those uninhibited, cute little kids performing in an exhuberant manner. As is customary with these programs, we had a shorter sacrament meeting, a total of 55 minutes. Following the meeting and completion of the tithing collection, I called my wife to tell her that I was coming home right away, reporting that "I'll be able to eat dinner with you and the children tonight." She was both excited and skeptical, "Are you sure?"

"Yes, I'm sure, I have no appointments at all!"

"Who is standing in the foyer?"

"No one."

"Well, when I see you walk in the door, I'll believe it." We hung up and I hurried out to my car. As I turned the corner I suddenly received a strong impression that Sister Blanchard needed my help. I was determined not to go. I said to myself, "I'll go after dinner!" But a strong answer said, "They need your help right now!" So I turned the car and started down the street toward their home. Then I saw Sister Blanchard walking down the street with tears streaming down her face. I stopped and she told me, "I was just on my way to see you. I need your help. I just have to get some advice and counsel."

After we talked for an hour and a half, I convinced her that the course she was pursuing would bring her great regret and sorrow. She agreed and said that she had just seemed to be powerless to alter what she was doing. She felt now she might be able to take steps to alleviate the problems.

As I went home I was received by an unhappy wife, "I knew someone would stop you," were her first words, "but you told me that you were coming home to dinner." I began to apologize and she asked, "Who stopped you?"

"Honey, it was the Holy Ghost." Her manner and face changed as she said, "That, I can understand. Why didn't you tell me that when you first walked in the door?"

* * * * * *

When I had been a bishop for just a short time a sister that I shall call Sister Gardner came in and posed a question to me: "What are the sins that cannot be forgiven?" I told her the two were murder and denial of the Holy Ghost.

"Can you be forgiven for moral transgression?" and when I said, "Yes you can." she continued, "I wanted to know that first before I told you." She then unraveled a story that was just heartbreaking. She had been involved sexually with three men for some time and said that she felt spiritually dead. She had even contemplated taking her own life. Now she asked, "Is it possible that I can repent and get back?"

I explained to her that it would take time and she must be humble and be willing to complete the steps of repentance. She had already recognized the wrong and felt very sad and unhappy about it and now she must make restitution. "How can I do that?" she asked. "I have taken nothing from anyone to restore to them."

"You have taken from them and yourself, your self-respect and self-esteem."

"But it was their idea in the first place and they were not virtuous before." With this I could agree. However, I pointed out to her that she had contributed to the problem and only she could make restoration for the part she had played in it.

"Oh, I don't know how I could go to them and ask their forgiveness." she cried.

"I would be glad to go with you, if you'd like, and to help you any way I can." I then asked her if she would like a blessing.

We waited, and we both fasted and prayed and then I gave her a blessing. She then told me, "Bishop, I can do it."

"I know you can, Sister Gardner." I answered, "I want you to know that I will be glad to go with you, if you wish."

"No, I must do it alone or not at all. It is better that way."

Later she told me what had happened as she called on the three young men. The first one, who was mighty surprised to hear her request for forgiveness, broke down and cried. He said, "I just didn't know anyone could feel that way—to ask for forgiveness to restore their self-respect. Everyone I know has been involved in the same behavior and thought it all right. I want you to know that I too would like to feel clean and find the self-respect you seek. I promise you that I will refrain from further sex activity until I am married."

The second young man, when he heard her plea for forgiveness that she might once again restore her feelings of self worth and self-respect, agreed and they parted as friends. The third story was a great deal different, but she persevered. The young man gave her a heated reply, "You want me to forgive you? For what? What's there to forgive? Everybody does it. I don't want your forgiveness and you're not getting mine. I'd do it again if I had the chance. What's with this Polly Puritan?"

She explained that she wanted peace of mind and spiritual release, and since he refused to accept her apology, she forgave him anyway. She bore witness of the truth of The Church of Jesus Christ of Latter-day Saints and parted from his company. Today she has been married in the temple, looks ten years younger and is a happy mother in Zion. It's exciting to see the Gospel in the lives of people like these and of others and to watch how the Lord helps and strengthens them.

Norman Gale

A Mission Call to the Spirit World

This second account is explained by its original title, which is: "An account of the circumstances of the death of Calvin Ray Cutler, born October 2, 1956 to Joseph Franklyn Cutler and Lorraine Ehninger Cutler, died January 30, 1976. Written by his father."

Friday, January 30, 1976 was an unusually nice day. A January thaw cleared the ground of snow and the early evening air was pleasant with just a light jacket on. Our oldest son, Greg, was due home from the Cumorah Mission in just three days and we were all feeling the excitement. Our other son, Calvin, seemed to be particularly excited. He had been working for many weeks redecorating the room that the two boys shared and for the last few days had been especially busy cleaning out and cleaning up. He seemed that day to glow with an air of anticipation. It was so contagious that his mother ran to him as he left on an errand and asked, "Cal, are you excited about Greg coming home?" He turned on his famous grin and called back, "Mom, I'm excited about everything!"

A bit later his mother was on the back porch shaking rugs to get the house spotless for Greg's homecoming when she heard sirens very close. She looked out on the patio, saw that the motorcycle was gone, and said to herself, "Oh, Cal, where are you?" Shortly after, the Bountiful, Utah police dispatcher advised me on the phone that Cal had been in an accident on his motorcycle and was in the hospital. My first reaction was exasperation rather than concern. Cal had always lived life fully and accidents were not uncommon. Before he was three years old he had cut off two fingers, broken his leg and eaten some drain cleaner, burning his mouth severely. In the three years he had been driving he had had some minor accidents, but had never been hurt seriously.

As we turned the corner on the way to the hospital, we could see the location of the accident just a couple of blocks from home. We could tell as we went by that this was likely serious. In the Bountiful hospital we were advised that he seemed to have a very serious brain injury. He was transferred to the care of a neurosurgeon in the cerebral intensive care unit of the LDS Hospital in Salt Lake City. My wife, Lorraine, our daughter, Jolayne, and I were joined there by our neighbors and Cal's closest friends, Ralph and Brigitte Wilcox, and also by the father and sister of the young man who had hit him. (The boy, a school chum of Cal's, was in shock, although not injured.)

When the doctor came in he told us that the prognosis was not good. He indicated that if Cal did survive there was a very little chance he would recover from the brain damage. His sweet mother (feeling, I am sure, the direction of the Lord) said to me, "We've got to let him go." We were told we could give him a priesthood blessing so we all knelt in prayer as I prepared myself for what I felt would be the most difficult administration I had ever performed.

As we went to his side we found him unconscious, unresponsive, and with labored breathing, but aside from some minor abrasions, unmarked from the accident. I had said earlier that I was certain the Lord would allow Cal to fulfill the mission intended for him. As I blessed him I was directed to promise that he would not suffer and that he would fill the mission chosen for him with the full use of his mind and all his faculties. We stood there for a few moments, said goodby and left the room. Ten minutes later his beautiful, powerful body and his beautiful sweet spirit had parted company in that experience we call death. When we were told this, the Spirit whispered gently that he had answered the call and that his mission had begun.

In the days and weeks following that night this same message was repeated countless times and in many ways. We became aware that we and some of his dearest friends had been partly prepared for this call home. Just a couple of nights before the accident, Lorraine had a dream in which someone in our family died just before Greg returned from his mission. In her dream many of the preparations for the funeral and other things were performed and the dream was clear enough for her to remember. Although she was not aware who it was, she thought on awakening that it must have been me. Also, Lorraine had worked with retarded children for several years and had seen the problems of brain injury there and with some of our friends who had suffered this kind of tragedy. On that same day she had been talking with some of those she worked with concerning this problem and had expressed the need to be willing to let a loved one go rather than pleading with the Lord to spare their life and perhaps have them suffer for years with these problems. It seems that she had been prepared to be able to let the Lord take him.

Our neighbor, Brigitte Wilcox, was very close to Cal. She was aware of the struggle Cal was having to develop the kind of testimony he felt he must have to go on a mission. He had postponed it for several months because he felt that he was not yet ready. She dreamed a few days before his death that he had received his mission call, but that for some reason people were not happy about it. She wondered at the time why there was such sadness at his mission call when we should have been so excited and happy.

One of his closest friends, Paul Olsen, wrote us, "When I heard the news about the accident, I was and still am shocked, hurt and unable to completely regain my composure. But I seemed to realize, even before talking to you this evening, that somehow it all seemed to fit." He told us of a dream he had a while before this happened. In the dream he and Cal were flying fighter planes in a war. He watched as a heat-seeking missile struck the plane Cal was flying and he awoke saying aloud, "Not Calvin, not Calvin!" When he learned of Cal's death this dream came forcefully to his mind. It was as though each who was so closely affected by his death were being prepared as much as possible to accept it.

A friend of my sister, whose son had been a missionary companion of Greg, told of her experience on the night Calvin died. "As I lay in the South Davis Hospital, in Bountiful, on January 30th, I could not keep the thought of the Cutlers from coming to my mind. I had spent the time reading the Book of Mormon and the Life of Hugh B. Brown. It had been a particularly spiritual day. About 8:30 a friend came to my room. We visited until the emergency buzzer rang through the building and he left. He had no sooner left than the Spirit of my Father in Heaven let me know that the injured person was a member of the Cutler family. My heart was full and my memory was vivid of the first time I had met this choice family. As I lay there waiting the return of my friend I was privileged to know that it was Calvin Cutler and to know that he would not live. As my friend returned to my room he was quiet and I said, 'Was that a motorcycle accident?' He replied, 'Yes.' Then I asked if it was Calvin Cutler. He just looked at me and said, 'How did you know?' I told him of my experience."

One of the earliest assurances we personally had that this was a call from the Lord was the calm comfort we had from the very beginning and through the following days. One experience occurred Sunday morning, the second day after his death. About six o'clock we both awoke gently and both felt very rested. It seemed to me that the room was lighter than usual for that time of morning and there was a feeling of peace and tranquility that we have rarely felt. For about an hour we talked and reminisced, laughed and cried, and began to understand. As we talked of problems Cal had faced in the last few months an experience of mine came to my mind and I was impressed that it was a type of the experience Cal had just passed through.

Several years before, I had experienced a rather extended period of depression. For several weeks I had been unable to lift myself from these feelings, which at times were so severe that I would feel that life was not worth continuing. I had tried to find what situations in my life or attitudes could cause those feelings and could find none. I finally concluded that the evil power of Lucifer had somehow taken hold of me, but I did not know why. One day as I felt I could no longer stand the struggle, I called aloud to the Lord in desperation and asked "Why?". Clearly and distinctly the Spirit spoke to my mind that I was to be called to serve in the Stake Presidency. I was assured that the test was over and almost instantly the dark, ugly depression was replaced by a sweet calm assurance. Two weeks later the call came as I had been told.

As we considered this experience we could recognize that Cal had also been through a great test in the last year or so of his life. We felt that he had passed the test and had answered his call just as I had answered mine. The evidence of that preparation and call which we recognized that Sunday morning was enough that we felt that the service planned for Tuesday should be approached more as a missionary farewell than a funeral. Because of this we felt that our Bishop, DuWayne Squire, (whose son, Brad, was one of Cal's closest friends and who himself was very close to Cal) should speak and that our next door neighbor, Ralph Wilcox, should also speak. Quite likely no one on earth had been as close to Cal as had Ralph in the last year or so. And finally we decided that since *we* had something so important to tell about our understanding of his death that I should be spokesman for us at the "Farewell". Bishop Squire had felt impressed that I should speak and was prepared to suggest this when we told him. Ralph had struggled with his emotions, knowing that we wanted him to speak, but felt that he must.

As Lorraine and I talked of these things that Sunday morning we felt that we ought not to stay home and mourn, but go to our meetings and share with others the sweet spirit that we felt. All through the day and for days afterward we felt the same calm assurance and strength that we felt that Sunday morning. We found in the next weeks that the understanding of his preparation we had received that morning was only the tip of the iceberg. Almost daily we received added knowledge and testimony of his preparation and call. We could not deny that the Spirit of the Lord, and Cal's spirit too, gave us strength.

The next day at the Farewell Service we felt the same spirit and Bishop Squire, Brother Wilcox and I all testified of the strength we felt there. I had an especially sweet experience as I spoke. I felt impressed to give a challenge to those present to live in harmony with the teachings of the gospel. I was about to say that this challenge was what Cal would give "if he were here," but as I began the phrase, I was strongly impressed that he was there near my side and said instead, "if he could speak".

During these days and for weeks after a story unfolded that we had only seen dimly as we had watched him in the months before. Some of it came from him through the things he left behind, and some came from his friends, employers, and other associates.

Calvin had always been actively involved in the church. All during his youth it was an assumed fact that he would someday serve a mission for the Lord. His older brother, Greg, had privately and quietly questioned the value of a mission, the importance of the gospel, had answered these questions for himself, then gone on with his preparation and into the mission field without seeming to miss a beat. We had assumed that Cal would do much the same, but he needed a different test for the mission he would be called to serve.

Shortly after he turned eighteen he was ordained an Elder in the Melchizedek Priesthood. Although he was worthy of this, he felt unprepared, apparently because he felt his testimony was not adequate. He felt very strongly that he could not rely on anyone else's testimony, but that he must know for certain himself that what he believed was true. Several months before his 19th birthday, which was on October 2, 1975, he made us aware that he would go on a mission only when he knew he was ready and not before. Much of the last year of his life seems to have been a testing, developing and refining of his testimony of the gospel.

Much of this was accomplished through a very sweet girl he met at the beginning of his senior year at high school. Sue White was a very pretty and popular girl. Though not a Latter-day Saint, she had strong religious attitudes and very high standards. Calvin was strongly attracted to her and his feeling became quite serious. He was torn, however, because of the differences in their beliefs. Although this didn't seem very important to her, it was of great concern to him.

They talked often of their beliefs and Cal found this very frustrating. He felt that, although he was sure he was right, he didn't have the knowledge, ability or assurance to convince her. He said once, "How can I go on a mission and talk with people about the church when I can't even answer her questions?" It seems in retrospect that this conflict was at the core of his trials.

As his birthday passed we sensed that he was struggling, but didn't then, and perhaps don't even now, understand the magnitude of that struggle. It seems that the end of the year and the beginning of the new one coincided with the ending of his testing and the beginning of the new phase of his life. Among the things we found in his "treasure box" after his death were some notes that he had written at great moments of trial or success. Each of these was listed as "1st Entry," or "3rd Entry," etc. with the date. Perhaps the most revealing of these was the last one, listed as *"Final Entry"* underlined and dated January 11, 1976, not quite three weeks before his death. It says in part, *"Final Entry;* The time has come where it is very necessary for me to make some very, very important decisions that will have a direct effect on my happiness for the future and the way I choose to live the rest of my life. I must now choose between the woman that I have loved very, very dearly for so long and have become so close to and the things that I know are right and best for me. I must do the things that are right....may I have the strength and courage to stand up for what is right!!!"

This signalled the final spurt of preparation for his "mission call." He accomplished more in those last two weeks, and particularly the last week before his death than he had ever done before. We knew he was busy, but we were amazed for weeks after as we found more and more that he had done during that time.

We knew he had spent much time in his room. We thought, and probably he did too, that he was just getting ready for Greg to come home. We found, though, that he had completely prepared his affairs for his death. Two or three years before he had made a "Treasure Box" and had in it his most prized possessions, records of his wrestling activities, school report cards, his girl friends, his work records, his tithing, his mission fund and many other things. He was a great record keeper and had condensed all these till he had in this treasure box the very essence of the most important things in his life. Also that night, for the first and only time in our recollection, he left the house without locking it, as though to say, "Here it is for you!"

We found that he had been busy elsewhere also. Apparently he had seen more of his friends in the last week than he had for months. He had visited all his grandparents within the last two days and been all around visiting with others. One of the prime topics of conversation was his upcoming mission. He had talked with Bishop Squire to set up a time to start processing his mission call. He visited a friend who worked in a clothing store and he browsed through "missionary suits." The morning of his death he told his employer that he would soon replace Greg in the mission field. Although he told these, and many others, that he was ready to go, he had not yet told us. It appears that he wanted to wait until his brother got home and then tell us all together.

He apparently tried even after his death to assist those close to him. He was very close to two girls; Sue White, who was not a member of the church, and Wendy Tingey. Each of these girls had a very real and impressive dream of him after he died. Wendy told us that in her dream the phone rang and when she answered it she recognized Cal talking. She asked him where he was and told him how much she missed him. He replied, "Don't worry. I'm happy!"

Sue, with whom he had discussed the church so much, wrote to us the following about her dream: I had heard from several people that Cal was alive and down at some wrestling meet. I was really excited and rushed right down. When I got there, however, I saw what I thought was Cal with another girl, sitting on the bleachers. I didn't know what to do. I wanted to rush over to him, but something held me back. I went over and sat on the far side of the bleachers, unsure what to do. Then Cal appeared beside me. This Cal was different somehow, not human. Oh, it looked like Cal; he even had his beard, but he had a sort of transparent look about him. It's hard to describe, but suffice to say that I knew he was still dead and not come back to life. I asked him about the other Calvin I had seen on the bleachers and he said very sternly, "That is not me." And then he told me that under no circumstances was I to talk to the other Calvin. All of a sudden I knew I had to ask Calvin which of our two religions was the true one. So I looked at him and said, "Cal, who was right, me or you?" He knew exactly what I was talking about and he said, "Sue, I was right about everything." I remembered being surprised even in my dream for I had fully expected a different answer. Then he said again, slowly, "I was right about *everything!*" There was so much more I wanted to say, but he said, "I can't stay, I must go." I wanted to have him stay so badly, but he again stressed he absolutely could not stay and he seemed preoccupied with something else on his mind. Then he was gone as suddenly as he had come.

Although we miss him tremendously, we have the assurance that he finished his preparation here among men and when ready, was called on his mission. During his life here on earth he influenced many people for good. Since he left us, he has continued to influence many for good here in this world, and we are sure, in the world of spirits.

Joseph F. Cutler

A Marine's Life Was Saved Through Prayer

In August 1942, when my brother, Belton Palmer, and I signed up in the Marine Corps in Phoenix, Arizona, we were told that we would be given assignments to different locations. Every time we transferred, he went one way and I went another. Later we both were sent to San Diego and were issued dog tags. They had P on them for 'protestant' and we told them we were not protestants, but that we were Mormons. They said that we were protestants and had to wear those dog tags. We scratched the P off and scratched an M in there. We don't know if anyone else knew if it stood for Mormon, Methodist or Mohammedan, but it satisfied us.

When we went overseas for the first time, we joined the fifth Marine Corp Division and trained at Camp Pendleton, California, then headed for Camp Tarawa in Hawaii. This is where we were notified that we were to head into combat. We went into the Captain and Major's office, and asked to see them. The Sergeant asked what kind of authority I thought I had, as a sergeant, to ask to see the Captain and the Major, both. I was quite sure they would see me because I was the boxing and judo instructor in the Marine Corp and they both worked out with me. Although they were superior officers they were also good friends. They both came to the door and I told them I wanted my dog tags changed. They were both good Catholics, and I knew that, so I asked them if they would change the dog tags designation for my brother and me and they said, "Your dog tags are marked protestant, aren't they?"

"Yes, but I'm not a protestant. I'm a Mormon."

"Well, that's protestant," the Captain replied.

"No, we're not protestants, we protest a lot of things the Catholic Church teaches, but we're not protestants. We were never a part of the Catholic Church, we're a separate and distinct religion."

"The rules forbid us to do that, Sergeant," he said, to which I replied, "How would you like to go into combat with a J or an H on your dog tags?"

The Major looked puzzled and said, "What's that?" and I said, "A Jew or a Hebrew." The Captain joined in with, "Well, we're not Jewish or Hebrew." and I answered, "And we're not protestants, we are L.D.S. and we want our dog tags marked." I tell you this because of something that happened later. We were then given dog tags marked L.D.S. We soon went aboard ship and knew we were headed for Iwo Jima.

While on board we held our own special church services and did not join in with the other church groups. One of the men asked us if we thought we were too good to join with them, so I said I would come up and I would join them. This day the man was talking on prayer, the Chaplain, it was. That was the most frustrating sermon I had ever heard. There he stood, shouting that if the boys could not pray, forget it, that he would pray for them. He said that even Christ's apostles couldn't pray. He said they should go through the war and if they'd do the fighting he'd do the praying.

After the sermon was over, I went up and challenged him "What made you think that Christ's apostles couldn't pray?" to which he answered, "Why do you think he gave them the Lord's Prayer?"

I replied, "If you'll look right above, the Lord tells you why—not to be as hypocrites to be seen of man, but to go into your closets and pray to God for the things you want."

I learned then that we didn't have to say too much before people knew we were Mormons. I had never talked to the Chaplain before and never seen him before but he said, "You're nothing but a damn Mormon and there's no use talking to you." There wasn't, but I don't know what I would have said then, nor do I know what I would say now if I was denied the right to pray to my Heavenly Father.

We landed on Iwo Jima the 19th of February, 1945. As I started up the beach there was a man, Sergeant Durkin, who brought his squad right alongside mine. I thought it might be wise to keep my brother, Belton, in reserve. He was also a squad leader. It seemed that everywhere I moved, the machine guns followed me, so Durkin came up and asked to be put in reserve because it seemed to him that everywhere I moved I was a target and he thought if he stayed close he'd get it too. So I brought Belton up to stay along with me.

On one occasion we were introduced to a large mortar we called "Leaping Lena." It looked like a telephone pole coming through the air and one heavy explosion came right over me, knocked me into the dirt, and completely covered me up. It knocked me unconscious for a period of time, I don't know for how long. The Lieutenant came by and saw where I had been and went back and told Belton I had been killed by the mortar. In the meantime I had struggled out of the dirt and gave him the O.K. signal that I so often gave when everything was all right. The amazing thing about it was that although Durkin had wanted to stay away from me, after this incident he felt that I was especially lucky and wanted to stay nearby. He said I must have luck of a special kind and he wanted to dig in near us.

On one occasion we were told by the Lieutenant to go take some flags down which were off to our left as the Japanese were taking a heavy toll on our Marine Corp. I said it was impossible. He said I would have to send some men over there because they were all pinned down. I went from hole to hole to ask the young men if anyone would volunteer and I saw the fear in their eyes. There was one old man of sixteen (I was the grandfather of 23); I just couldn't get them to go. I went back and asked Belton if he would go with me and he said he'd go wherever I asked him to. We again knelt in that foxhole and asked our Heavenly Father to bless us to do what we had to do. We decided to leave my rifle behind; he would take his rifle and I would go ahead and he would try to cover me. We proceeded to the flags. The amazing thing was as we climbed out of our foxhole, it was as though someone had turned the lights off in a room—all the firing stopped for the first time in several days on the island. We went and cut the flags down and returned to our holes, and as though that had been the signal for the firing to start again, the firing started and we thanked our Heavenly Father that he had answered our prayers so directly.

A couple of nights later, Durkin again jumped in the hole with us as we were praying. He asked our forgiveness for interrupting us, but he would have interrupted us no matter when he came. I had often said in a joking manner, that the Lord had no time to answer anyone else because we kept him so busy, night and day. Durkin said that's what he had come for, to ask us to teach him how to pray. I kiddingly said, "We thought everyone knew how to pray." To which he replied, "I don't even know the words to say." We explained that a prayer must be a personal thing and each individual prayed for the things he needed and wanted. We tried to teach him how to pray; to address Heavenly Father first, then thank him for his blessings. He said, "What in heavens name do I have to be thankful for?"

I explained to him that he had his life, and some of the friends who had landed on the Island with us a few days before, and that we were fighting on foreign soil and not having our families and homes destroyed by bombs. Also we should be thankful that we were Americans. We went on to tell him that he should then ask for what he wanted and then close in the name of Jesus Christ, Amen.

An amazing thing happened the next morning as we were moving up to attack. All of a sudden Durkin, who had been lying flat firing at the enemy, jumped up and ran to us saying, "He does, he does, he does!" I said "Who does? And does what?" Excitedly he replied, "God does hear and answer prayers." I said "Of course he does." Then he told me that a Japanese mortar had landed between his arms and face and hadn't gone off. He was praying at the time for the first time in his life. Some of the Marines made fun of him and said, "Oh, it was just a dud." Well, you couldn't convince Durkin that it wasn't an answer to his prayer and you couldn't convince me that it wasn't an answer to his prayer either.

A few days later the Lieutenant said I had to go take a pillbox. I was to get near the pillbox and blow it up because they were having crossfire and couldn't get out. I told the Lieutenant it was impossible and told him to see if we couldn't get some heavy mortar to help out, but he said that we couldn't. It wasn't mine to wonder why, it was mine to do or die. I passed word along to my men that they were not to come out until I signalled them. So I started to run and here they came right alongside me. I again ordered them not to come until I could find a place for them to come to, with some cover for them, and said I'd figure how to get to the pillbox. I began to run again. I finally found a bomb crater and dived into it. As I did so the machine gun started to sashay across the top of the crater. I knew I had to signal the platoon or they would be coming after me and as I raised up out of the crater the machine gun fire caught me in the head and neck and chest and back and I was hurt very badly. They began to pepper me with knee mortars and I began to beg the Lord for my life. When I tried to yell to my men I found I was paralyzed and I could not talk. I again prayed very hard. I could feel my life slipping from me and I felt to pray further. I asked the Lord to spare me to return home to my family; I promised him many things, that I would be a better man, a better husband, a better father, a better member of the church. As I talked to him with all my heart and with the depth of my soul, begging for the gift of life, an assurance came into my soul that everything was going to be alright. I soon began to be able to speak again, though I was completely paralyzed on my left side.

Back with the others, Belton said he was going to go out and over to where I was, but the Lieutenant told him that he had seen the machine gun fire hit me just as I raised up to yell, so it was no use to go because I was dead. Belton broke loose and came up with me and jumped into the hole with me, though this was deemed to be an impossible task to get through that area. He asked me how I was and I said, "Alright." and he replied, "Yeah you look alright." The only thing I had left of my pack was my consecrated oil, my Book of Mormon and my Bible, the rest was torn to shreds. I was wounded in several places, so Belton gave me first aid and administered to me and then went back and got a navy corpsman to help him. I had been wounded at about 8:00 in the morning and at 2 or 3 in the afternoon we tried to run out, with one of them on each side of me.

From the time I was hit and for several weeks afterwards, I was conscious and unconscious, and it was really a traumatic experience. When I was being carried down to the ship I saw the flag and I was thrilled and delighted, because I had not known if I would ever see the flag again. There it flew on Serabachi Mountain and I choked up as I thought of what it stood for. I get very angry at people who do not appreciate and respect the flag and all that it means to us as Americans.

They put me on a hospital ship to move me to Guam. I lay on board in a hospital bed in the room where all the boys lay who had been shot through the chest. They put plasma into both arms, they tried to bandage up my back, but as I would breathe, the air would go right on out my back through the wounds. I was having trouble breathing, was losing blood, and was alternately conscious and unconscious until I lost much track of time.

I don't know when it was that the doctor came by and offered me something to drink, saying "Take this for shock." I asked what it was and when he told me it was rum, I told him, "I don't need that." In answer he said, "Well, you are going into shock and if you do, you don't have any chance." I told him I didn't need it, that the Lord had seen me this far and he would see me the rest of the way. The reaction of the doctor amazed me—he stood back and yelled, "Boy, I've always heard about the obnoxious Marine Corp, how they always won all the wars themselves, how the Navy never did anything at all, that the Marines did it all. Not only do we have a big tough Marine Corp sergeant who's done all the fighting, we have one that's favored of God. The rest of you guys have taken rum but he doesn't need it because the Lord's going to take care of him." And then they made fun of me as they took other drinks and soon they were drunk and the next day we saw several of the boys buried at sea. Whether the drinking had anything to do with it, I don't know, but I do know that the Lord didn't give me the excuse to drink, and I didn't avail myself of the excuse.

I was taken down to Guam and there I'll never forget the experience. As the men were carrying me on a stretcher they mumbled about how heavy I was. A little nurse came to cut the clothes off my body and she handled me like a toothpick and I was surprised that she did not complain about my weight. I lost track of time again and once again was conscious and unconscious. One time I heard a voice say, "Is there anyone here that is a Mormon?" and I listened as the little nurse said, "Yes, I noticed a young man whose tags were marked L.D.S." and she brought him to me. I was so grateful that I had gone to bat and got our dog tags marked L.D.S. because he came over and stuck his hand out saying, "I'm Reed A. Johnson from Salt Lake City. Are you a Mormon?" I said, "Boy, am I! And I'd sure like to be administered to." That afternoon he and Chaplain Jackson came and administered to me.

A few days later as I lay there with some degree of consciousness, the doctor came in and started to check my record. He asked why they hadn't changed the record since that guy was dead. The nurse assured him that I was there and still alive when he said, "Good Lord, go stop that!" He had sent word that I was dead to my company and my brother, Belton, who was wounded and was hospitalized elsewhere. I was grateful to the Lord that my life had been spared.

When I came back to the United States, I found people who did not want to shake my hand because they thought I had been killed in Iwo Jima. Even the doctor had said that there was no way I could have lived because of the serious wounds I sustained.

I am so grateful and thankful to the Lord for his care and help, for I know without his inspiration, his guidance and his help in many other ways, especially his answers to my prayers at the height of the battle, I would not have returned to my home and family in Utah.

J. Duffy Palmer

He Saw the Savior and His Future Mission

Special things began to happen to Ensyne S. Clark when he was about 17 years old. That was in 1951 while he was living in Roosevelt, Utah, shortly before the family moved back to Salt Lake City. The "thing" that happened to him was the most unusual gift of being able to sense what others were going to say, just before they spoke. He wondered why this gift was given to him, but he humbly accepted it, hoping that he would use it wisely. That was the first gift.

He graduated from high school and entered Utah State University in the fall of 1952. As the summer of 1953 approached and he neared his 19th birthday, he strongly felt the spirit of the Lord working on him. He was filled with a desire to study the scriptures more seriously. He wished that he was better prepared for a mission although he had a pretty fair grasp of doctrine at that time.

Because of the Korean conflict and the subsequent limiting of missionaries, he was asked to wait a year, until he was 20, but finally he received his mission call in July, 1954 to the Northern States Mission. He was to enter the mission home August 20th. He continued to study the Book of Mormon, the Pearl of Great Price, and the Doctrine and Covenants.

On July 27, 1954, he drove his car to the Logan Temple to receive his endowments. When he entered the temple, the temple president, President George Raymond, called him into his room and said, "Elder Clark, I promise you, in the name of the Lord Jesus Christ that you *will* go on your mission. I wish I had a room in this temple where you could stay." Ensyne was very puzzled by these statements, they made him most uncomfortable. What could they mean? Before the evening was over President Raymond had repeated them a second and third time, to Elder Clark's amazement. What was the meaning of "you *will* go on your mission"? Wasn't that already understood? He had his mission call, didn't he?

President Raymond asked him to speak to the congregation in the chapel before the session began. He remembers speaking to the group and wondering as they arose and came and stood before him as he spoke. Afterwards he could not remember a word that he had said. Following his endowment session, President Raymond asked him to *stay* in the temple. He completed two more sessions and was then asked to participate in some sealing ordinances. At the conclusion of these ordinances the group lingered to hear President Raymond say, "I wish this young man could stay in the temple." And turning to Elder Clark he once again repeated, "I promise you in the name of Jesus Christ, that you *will* go on your mission."

As Elder Clark left the Logan Temple it was about 10:40 p.m. and he was more puzzled than ever about the things the temple president had said. As he pulled out of the parking lot to drive back to Salt Lake, his mind became a blank and he was not aware of his surroundings, nor conscious of driving the car, until he arrived safely at home. It was as though he had been driven home by some unseen power. Could there be any connection between this happening and the almost fearful words of the temple president? Would he have had an accident?

He was engaged to a young lady who lived in Vernal, Utah. He went August 9th to say his farewells to her. While driving back to Salt Lake after midnight, he had an automobile accident which they reconstructed to have been caused by his falling asleep at the wheel of the car. When the highway patrol found him, someone had been there before them and had looted his wallet, removing several hundred dollars of his missionary funds. He was taken to the hospital in Heber City and remained unconscious for 14 days.

During this period, following the accident, he would often quote from the Book of Mormon and would even sing church songs as he lay in an unconscious state. When he regained consciousness, he was once more at home and could not understand immediately why he was in pajamas in mid-afternoon. He was told of his accident and of how the Lord had spared his life following several administrations. Then it was that he told of the marvelous happenings that he had experienced during this time. He saw his mission to the Northern States from beginning to end. He knew the places where he would labor. He saw the people and was even given names of many. He was told of some of the conversions and baptisms that would occur. Later, they all proved to be exactly as he had seen them in the vision he had experienced.

He also witnessed his own death as it was to be at some future date. The vision as he beheld it: he saw himself driving across a bridge from Omaha, Nebraska to Council Bluffs, Iowa and watched the car plunge off the bridge into the river. Soon he saw men dragging the river for his body. He then witnessed his spirit sitting up on the bluffs watching the searchers. (To this day he avoids that bridge whenever possible.)

At one time a glorious light appeared to him with a whiteness that was "whiter than white" and in the light he saw the Lord, even Jesus Christ. The Savior's identity was testified to him in that instant. As he gazed in wonderment, a feeling of great sadness came over him because Jesus wept. The scene was replaced immediately as he witnessed the Savior on the cross. At the foot of the cross were many people who were weeping because of the evil in the world. He knew many of the people, he said (and he later told the author), "You were there, Aunt Norma." Then he saw the earth encompassed in darkness, but just off to his left, just out of the line of vision appeared a shaft of white light, like that which he had seen when he had briefly glimpsed the Savior. Once again he felt a great sorrow because of the wickedness of the people of the world.

During his mission he labored one month in Des Moines, Iowa, then was transferred to Harrin, Illinois for six months. While there he knocked on the door of a house and when a man came to the door, said, "Hello, Mr. Fox" to which Mr. Fox replied, "I've been waiting." Several sisters in Nebraska and Iowa came into the church as he had been told during his coma. One sister was unable to get permission from her husband so she could be baptized, but she was converted to the church, had a testimony, and desired baptism. Another sister, after many problems with her husband pertaining to her baptism finally, with Elder Clark's help, obtained permission from her husband and was then baptized. Yet another joined after he left town. He had not been concerned, for as he said, "I *knew* that she would."

He saw in the vision that he would go first to Omaha and then be sent to Columbus, Nebraska to help organize a branch. There he would be made branch president and supervising elder. He was to help organize a branch in Norfolk also, and these things came about as he knew they would.

When he was moved to Council Bluffs, Iowa as supervising elder, he felt the presence of the adversary very strongly. At one time, after they had retired for the night they heard a door close and a voice saying, "Deny that Jesus is the Christ!" Louder and louder it was repeated in his ear, so he jumped out of bed. He felt a strong evil feeling in the room at the same time. There were six missionaries living in the house at the time and one of them, an Elder Owens, who was in the same room with Elder Clark, was thrown to the floor. His eyeballs were rolling and he was struggling. The missionaries laid their hands on him and cast out the evil spirit. This they followed with a prayer circle, beseeching the Lord to cast the devil out of the house. There seemed to be a reprieve from that evil feeling as the devil departed from their home. Shortly afterwards they also began having much success in their work.

Returning to Elder Clark's recital of his experiences while unconscious, he said that he had received a vision which disturbed him somewhat. He had been told that he would marry a young lady named Barbara that he would meet in Waterloo, Iowa. To a young man engaged to a young lady that he had dated for nearly seven years this was disturbing news indeed. Although he was willing to do what the Lord wanted, he was somewhat resentful at the thought of breaking his engagement to his childhood sweetheart.

When the time came in his mission that he was transferred to Waterloo, Iowa, he looked up Branch President Sagers and said to him, "Where does Barbara live?" to which President Sagers replied, "Which Barbara?" He then told him that her father was a dairy farmer. He answered, "She lives four or five miles out of town." There followed a detailed description which he and his companion, Elder Baker, followed. They arrived at the family farm to find that Barbara had just had an accident. She had slipped in the milk parlor and was unconscious and in bed. After they administered to her, there followed a friendly get-acquainted visit with Barbara and her mother. They were both very active in the church, although not baptized members at the time. Her father had declined to give permission for their baptismal. Barbara was branch organist and had paid a faithful tithe for more than a year prior to this time. She was a very friendly person and was thought of very highly in the branch. Elder Clark counselled her not to be too friendly with the missionaries. When he and his companion left, she turned to her mother to say, "That is the man that I am going to marry." In spite of his stern treatment of her (he still carried a bit of resentment) she saw in him a special spirit which she strongly admired.

When his mission was completed and he was released, on October 27, 1956, he went to see Barbara and asked if he might date her when he completed a short tour of his mission. She agreed. When he returned November 3rd after he had visited many other members, performed a baptism, and received his official release, he took her to a show. He remembers the movie: War and Peace. They sat on opposite sides of the car seat. The next night they went bowling and arrived home at 12:20 a.m. As they sat a moment in the car he said to her, "I'm going to ask you to marry me..." to which she replied, "What time is it?" He told her, "It is 12:20." She said, "Tell me when it is 12:30." When the time had passed, he said, "It is now 12:30." She slipped over and put her arm around him and kissed him on the cheek and said, "The answer is yes!"

This schooled, disciplined, missionary trembled. He was disturbed. Somewhat guiltily, with his heart in his throat, he kissed her goodnight and went back home to the elders. The next day, November 6th, he went to bid her goodbye, kissed her and then headed for home. After a brief correspondence, he returned, baptized her and they were married. They now have a beautiful family of six adopted and sealed children. One is waiting for them in the spirit world. They now live in Tempe, Arizona.

In January of 1977, an outstanding miraculous experience further attested to the many "things" that have happened to Elder Clark: One day while driving in Tempe, he was waiting to make a left turn when he saw a truck rapidly heading right at him. The driver apparently was unaware that he was in a left-turn lane. A crash was imminent. Prayerfully, Brother Clark raised both hands, palms forward, and moved them over to the left, as if pushing the truck over into the other lane. The truck moved sideways as his hands moved over to the left and a serious accident was averted. He was and is humbly grateful to the Father for sparing his life once again, through a miracle.

EPILOGUE

He loves us! What a tremendous boost this knowledge can give us. He loves us even when we sin, but he sorrows then too, that our progress and joy are retarded. As our obedience to His commandments increases and we yearn to serve Him and our fellow men, we are bringing ourself into the position which makes it possible for our Heavenly Father to increase His help to us.

To gather this collection of my brother's and sister's (as well as my own) stories of the Father's help to His children has been a choice and rare experience. As I talked to friends, relatives, and acquaintances, I was overwhelmed to find how fantastically active, on our behalf, that the Father has been. My gratitude, my love and appreciation of "His caring" for us increased astronomically as this living proof of His frequent assistance in our lives became more apparent. My desire is to share this marvel with others, so that they might desire closer, more active contact with Him, that they might give greater praise to the Father and know the joy of working with Him.

The love that is shown to us by the Father and His Son, Jesus Christ, is totally beyond our comprehension, yet we can be blessed with enough knowledge and appreciation of that love that we can rejoice and be humbly grateful for it. We can value it so highly that we will endeavor to share it with others, that they too may know the happiness that living the Gospel brings.

There is proof in the experiences recounted in this book that the Father is watching over us daily and doing what he can for us, within the framework of free agency, to lead us back to Him. Our willingness to be obedient to the commandments, all of the commandments, is the key to joy and happiness and a closeness with our Father that truly places our hand in His. With this awareness, we can arise daily, knowing that He is beside us, giving us whatever help and guidance that we need. His loving and caring is surely our Salvation: we can know that His love is everlasting!

INDEX